# "MY MA MA"

## THE INSPIRING STORY OF AN ORPHAN

## GIVEN THE CHANCE TO HAVE A LIFE

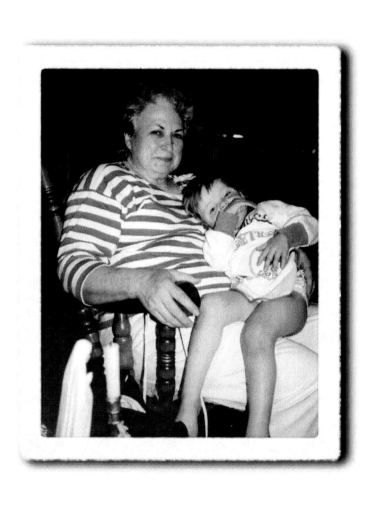

# "MY MA MA"

## AN INSPIRING STORY OF AN ORPHAN

## GIVEN THE CHANCE TO HAVE A LIFE

Betty Genter

*Betty Genter*

DIGITAL
LEGEND

2010

For additional copies visit: www.digitalegend.com/catalog

Send inquiries to:
Digital Legend Press and Publishing
1994 Forest Bend Dr.
Salt Lake City, UT 84121
U.S.A.

For info write to: info@digitalegend.com
or call toll free: 877-222-1960

Printed in the United States of America
First Printing: July 2010 (V1)

ISBN: 978-1-934537-89-3

## DEDICATION

This book is a labor of love, dedicated to Alexandra and every
natural and adoptive parent who has survived all the changes
encountered along the way to growing up. The journey of life
goes on.

# TABLE OF CONTENTS

# PREFACE

Adopting a child, especially at an older age, comes with its own unique set of challenges. In the process of loving, giving, and guiding Alexandra, as she grew from toddler to an adult, many similarities and parallels between her and me became apparent.

As I prepare the format of this book, I realize I am writing about her, but find her writing has to be a part of her story. Using her words makes her story more real and provides insight into who she is becoming. Her thoughts show how life is always changing and that we are on this journey together.

# 1

## THE JOURNEY BEGINS

*The sun was just rising in the east; hot and humid, as my husband and I shifted our cramped positions in the rear of our Ford Taurus station wagon. It was the dawning of July 31, 1992 and we were in the parking lot at JFK International Airport in New York. We had left our home between Rochester and Buffalo at approximately 10:00 pm the night before to avoid daytime traffic or other delays such as construction. Realizing we would arrive early, we were prepared to take a nap in the early morning. With the seats down, some pillows, a blanket, and an air mattress, we were able to rest for a few hours before grabbing some breakfast in the airport and before heading for the Lufthansa terminal.*

*It seemed to be the end of a long journey of paperwork and waiting, but in reality, we knew it was just the beginning of the journey... a journey to give love, hope, and a future to Alexandra.*

This journey actually began on a windy, rainy Friday evening, October 5, 1990. Our son, Joseph, was a senior in high school and would soon be off to his first year at college, there were no more foster children occupying our four- bedroom colonial brick house. After retirement from my thirty-four years as a teacher and then an administrator with the Albion Central School District, in October of 1990, I was beginning to want more of a challenge. Retirement was great. Lots of time to do all the things I did not have time for with my busy school schedule. I started searching for something to do part-time. After reading an advertisement in the paper for a part-time director of a back-to-work program at nearby Genesee Community College, I decided to apply. I interviewed. Being a school administrator, a person needs to have excellent organizational and programming skills, as well as be able to work well with people. I was hired.

It was good to be working again: setting up workshops and bringing in speakers on different job-related topics. As coordinator for the SOS Program, I enjoyed contacting people to fit into our workshops and as Friday of the first week of my new job arrived; I was tired from all the week's organizing.

I curled up on the sofa in our den and turned on the television to the 20/20 Program, "Nobody's Children." It was a follow-up to an April 1990 story on American couples trying to adopt Romanian children. The program had generated more than 25,000 letters by viewers; the most of any segment in the series history. The whole program was on the plight of Romanian children. It was reported that thousands of children had been discarded by the state: "rejected and left to die in warehouses for what's called the deficient and the unsalvageable." There were many pictures of children tied to their cribs, sharing their bed with several others, lying in their wet, soiled rags; many were sick and needed medical attention. My own comfortable surroundings in contrast to these poor, helpless children brought out a fountain of tears I couldn't stop, cascading down my cheeks, as I continued to watch the images of hopelessness coming from the wide-eyed, hungry children. After a few minutes, I called my husband to come and look at this program. By the end of the one-hour program, I was saying something like: "Here we are, retired from good jobs, living in a big house, full of children's toys, furniture and books; and there they have nothing. Most of all, they had no hope for a future. Those who needed medical help were already handicapped with no medical attention, no good food, and no education." Numbers were given as to how many orphans faced this kind of future in the hundreds of children's homes in Romania. At the end of the broadcast, there was an address to write to if you wanted information about international adoption and a list of agencies dealing with international adoptions. I sent for the information.

Many phone calls to agencies ensued. At the same time, I read and collected every article I could find in magazines and newspapers that dealt with international adoption. I was about to journey into an area I knew nothing about.

The stories abounded about the terrible conditions in Romania, about the corruption involved; the bribes. One article stated: "An estimated 40,000 to 100,000 Romanian orphans are products of the forced population growth plan of executed leader Nicolae Ceausescu. His campaign was to increase Romania's population from 23 million to 30 million by the year 2000. Many infants and young children are malnourished, often left alone in filthy conditions, and suffer physical and mental disabilities." World Vision had committed millions annually for three years to help save those children who could be saved. Dr. Barbara Bascom, a pediatrician and child-development expert and her husband, a surgeon, moved from their Maryland home to Romania to work with World Vision in the orphanages. In one article, she describes her experience when she first arrived:

There was room after room chock-full of old metal cribs with wire mesh. Paint peeled from the walls, and there was a sickening smell of urine, which soaked many of the mattresses. The smallest babies were swaddled so tightly to protect against the chill of the rooms that they could hardly move. All you could see was their eyes. They lived in their cribs. They had no toys; they never went outside.

After much collecting of information from thirteen agencies, Illien Adoptions International of Atlanta, Georgia was chosen as the agency with which I felt most comfortable. My husband and I decided that we would like a family of older children, with at least one of them being a girl. Much paperwork began. A home study, INS forms, state forms, physicals for each member of our family, fingerprinting, background checks, financial statements, and much more. A sheet of "Documents Needed" stated:

First, contact the Immigration and Naturalization Service and request an I-600 Package. It will contain forms and three sets of fingerprint cards. Contact an adoption agency to begin the Home Study. If you want to adopt more than one child, make sure the home study says that you are approved for more than one child. Documents needed for INS for unknown child:

1.  Certified Birth Certificates of adoptive parents

2.  Proof of US citizenship

3.  Proof of termination of previous marriages

4.  Home Study with attached recommending the proposed adoption, signed by an official of state agency

5.  Fingerprint cards

6.  Certified copy of Adoption Agency's license

7.  Proof of employment security, stating position and salary on company letterhead

8.  Copy of latest 1040 form, notarized.

We were officially approved for adoption in the spring of 1991. The whole process was actually hurried because we held a New York State Department of Social Services Certificate to Board Children reissued on 3/30/90, as we had been foster parents to six foster children throughout the previous fifteen years. We had our international home study completed by Marge Stevens from Hillside Children's Center in Rochester… an amazing person! Adoption was an important part of Marge's life, both personally and professionally. Not only was she the Director of Adoption at Hillside, she also is the mother of 17 children: 13 of them adopted, and four biological children. She has placed more than 1200 Children in the 24 years of working with adoptions. At Hillside she provided adoption preparation and post-placement services for international and special needs adoptions, along with studies for domestic adoptions.

## A LONG TREK

Part of the contract with the agency stated that they would search until they found the child (children) the family wanted. Throughout the summer, the agency began sending pictures of Romanian children ready for adoption. We kept rejecting them because of their gross physical problems. We felt because we were older, that we could not deal with the severe health issues most of the children presented in the pictures. Some had just been released from the hospital with AIDS (from contaminated blood transfusions, given for any illness), others were listed as a family, but had different fathers; others were severely handicapped. After rejecting five sets of pictures, I read in the newspaper the following: "In December of 1989 Romanian orphanages were thrown open and the country quickly became a baby mill for would be adoptive parents … the Romanian government has said it will suspend adoption proceedings starting tomorrow while it reorganizes operations." There were more stories about people from many countries going to Romania and just kidnapping children; as well as parents selling their children. All of our correspondence with Illien International ceased for a while. I was sure that we would not be getting the family of children we wanted.

## ALMOST FORGETTING

As I organized workshops and set up seminars for my job at the college, I began to forget about the agency's promise to find the right child for us. I did not hear any more from Romania. Then, in the first week of December 1991, came a telephone call from Illien Adoptions. "How would you like a little girl from Russia?" After asking how old she was and hearing she was only three years, nine months, I thought about it and said, "No, because of our age, she is too young." The woman at the other end said if I changed my mind, they could overnight a video of her to us. When my husband came home, I told him how surprised I was to hear from the agency. It had been a long time and they were now dealing with an orphanage in Moscow, Russia... Also, that they had a video of a girl which we could view. He surprised me when he said, "It wouldn't hurt to look at it. Why don't you send for it?"

## THE JOURNEY MOVES ON

The video arrived in two days and we watched it repeatedly. We showed it to our friends. It was simply amazing how much she looked like children on my husband's side of the family (German). The write-up, which came with her, was somewhat questionable and contradictory. Realizing translation from Russian to English, in itself, could create problems with descriptions and conditions; I studied the background report sent to us with the video.

It said that Alexandra Kornilova had been at Moscow's Children's Home #25 since shortly after her birth. Her

mother, a 38-year-old single bookkeeper, did not want the child and had attempted an unsuccessful abortion, which resulted in Alexandra's premature birth. She weighed 2.8 pounds and measured 15 inches long at birth. Alexandra was diagnosed with "Spastic Paralysis", stiffness in the joints and ligaments of the legs. She had some delay in psychomotor and speech development. Another paper from the agency said she had mild cerebral palsy, affecting her lower extremes and that she was developmentally slow. A translated certificate dated 6/17/1992 states:

This is given to certify that in the book of birth registration, kept by Tsaritsinskiy district registry of the city of Moscow there is a record No. 3514 made on May 20, 1988 on the birth of a child:

KORSHUNOVA ALEKSANDERA ALEKSANDROVICH

Date of birth: Feb. 16, 1988

Mother: KORSHUNOVA NADEZHDA NIKOLAYEVNA

Father: KORSHUNOV ALEKSANDER NAUMOVICH *

*Spelling is very changeable and it is hard to determine the correct spelling.

In the video, I saw a little girl, who looked like a toddler just beginning to walk. She had to hold the hands of the women aides who cared for the children in the orphanage. She managed to move around the room, which held eight other children her age, by holding on to tables and chairs; all the while standing on her toes like a ballerina. She did not say much during the filming. When asked a question in Russian, she replied clearly in Russian. At one point, she pointed toward the window and spoke at length about a bird she had seen in the tree outside. Her way of watching and observing the other children at play told me that she was not developmentally slow.... actually quite the opposite. The playroom appeared clean, with a small bookshelf where a few toys were kept. There were small, child-sized tables and chairs.

I took the video to Dr. Matthew Landfried in Batavia, an orthopedic surgeon, and asked if he and his wife would watch it and let me know what they thought. The message back to me was what I already knew in my heart. "She is the worst she will ever be... it is not progressive. CP affects the motor control of the muscles from the brain. In her case, a specific part of the brain does not work well on her lower extremities. CP is caused by birth trauma where the blood supply is interrupted to a body part. It is not inherited. Her problem can easily be corrected with minor surgery where hip and heel cords are lengthened and braces are worn." Both the doctor and his wife thought she was very functional for her age, that her responses were age-appropriate, and, like me, thought that she certainly was not mentally slow; quite the opposite. They suggested Shriner's Hospital in Erie, PA, for correction of her problem. Their final comment made a deep impression on me at the time and resurfaces even now, "The real question you must ask yourself, is, 'Can you accept her, as she is, even if nothing could be done to help improve her condition?'"

Now fast forward to her high school years. Alex became interested in health care as her life work. As part of her course work at Notre Dame High School (Health Careers), she was sent to shadow in Dr. Landfried's office. Imagine his surprise when she told him who she was and how he had first met her. Amazing!

My chiropractor, upon hearing of my desire to adopt Alexandra and then viewing the picture of her, suggested that I call "Richard" who had a son working in Russia for the US government. Everyone was concerned that I was about to take on more than I could handle. Richard said he would give the information I had regarding Alexandra to his son, and that his son, would be glad to visit the orphanage and check on her and her surroundings. The message came back that the women who cared for the children were kind and clean. There were very few toys for the children. Everything seemed clean and orderly. Food was scarce, but most of the children looked healthy, even though they never went outside. We had kept the tape for almost a week. It was time to make the big decision.

## A Prayerful Decision

On December 8, 1991, we formally accepted the child and the challenge named, Alexandra. December 8th is the Feast of the Immaculate Conception in the Catholic Church. Later, when Alex was in 7th grade and had become a very good writer, she was asked to share her story in a newspaper. It was entitled: "STORY OF AN ABORTION SURVIVOR and why her Dad faithfully comes to our Rosary Marches and Prayer Vigils."

In Alex's words:

> *My name is Alexandra. I was born in Moscow, Russia 2 months premature with Cerebral Palsy and weighed only 2 ½ lbs. I was supposed to be dead--not alive-- because my mother tried to abort me by using an illegal drug, but for some reason she did not succeed. I will not hold this against her because she lived in a small apartment with her sick father. Therefore, she could not afford to have me. After birth, I was put in a government-operated orphanage with other children. The nurses there were good and took good care of us, but the meals were meager and consisted mostly of soups. I could not walk until I was three and only then with much difficulty on my toes. When I was four, the government decided that the most severely handicapped children could be adopted out to people from other countries. Through this intervention I came to the United States of America in July of 1992 to a new home in Albion, New York. I adjusted well. After some time I had a few operations on my legs and feet. Now I am 12 years old and I am in the 7th grade at St. Mary's School in Batavia. If my birth mother had succeeded in aborting me, I would not be standing here today...the horrors of abortion!*

## THE WAITING BEGINS

The Russian government was in a state of disarray and confusion after Communism failed and no longer ruled. In 1987, President Ronald Reagan had visited Berlin, Germany, and urged Soviet leader, Mikhail Gorbachev, to tear down the Berlin Wall. In September of 1989, the Hungarian government opened the border for East German refugees and in November 1989, the Berlin Wall was opened, and Communism fell. In 1991, government facilities and offices were undecided on policy and often changed the rules. At first, we were told one of us would have to go physically to Russia to adopt Alexandra in a Russian court. Therefore, I gave notice to my employer, Genesee Community College, that I would need a leave of absence for a month. At the same time, I prepared for the trip. It was January, so warm clothes and a snowsuit were purchased. Then a message came from Illien Adoptions that the government had changed its mind. We would now have a choice of whether we would go personally to Russia or pay an extra fee for the agency to escort Alex to America. It would have been nice to actually visit her homeland, but after considering everything, we decided to have her escorted to New York by the agency.

The wait was long. Spring came, then summer. Many more papers were filled out and sent to our agency. A proxy attorney had to act for us in the Russian court. A visa and passport had to be obtained for Alex through the American consulate after she was given a clean bill of health. Each month I waited for the arrival date to appear in our mailbox. During this time, I prepared for her arrival: readying her room, buying clothes, and contacting doctors for options for fixing her legs.

I kept thinking that something would happen to postpone the date of arrival even further into the summer. Finally, the letter arrived. I tore open the agency letter and there it was: July 31, 1992.

## BACK TO JFK

It was finally July 31. The plane was scheduled to arrive at 11:00 am. The plane, Aeroflot flight #315, did not arrive until 3:00 pm. The waiting room assigned to the waiting adoptive parents, relatives, interpreters, reporters, and Illien personnel began filling up quickly and as the waiting and arrival time got closer, the noise level increased. Some people held flowers, gifts, and balloons. The heat of the day and the bodies in the room increased, as I stared impatiently at the sign over the double doors, "CUSTOMS." Balloons waved back and forth across the front of the sign as I silently prayed and wondered, "Are they ever going to land, or is all this an illusion?"

Then at 4:40 pm someone opened the double doors and in came a group of three adult women and four baby-like children, (three were seated in carriers similar to grocery carts—they were boys). They looked to be only one or two years old, but I knew they were all four years old. One boy had a heart defect. One had a harelip; the other a cleft palate.

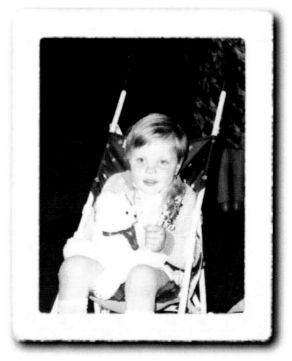

Then there was Alexandra, holding on to the hand of her nurse from Russia, the one who was in the video, Letha Co-stanza. She was struggling to walk on her toes in shoes that were too small. The shoes were green and yellow sandals. Her dress was a baby dress with puff sleeves in a green and white stripe and on her legs were stockings, gray in color, and at least a size 4 or 5, so large that they were pulled way up and rolled under her armpits. For a minute, the room became extremely quite as everyone looked at the arriving group. A boy named Alex, had no roof in his mouth and could not talk. However, like all the other parents in different parts of the country, Alex's parents had already arranged with their physicians to correct his defect. He would be living in Hamburg, New York, near Buffalo. He and Alexandra were the only children to go home from JFK. The other children had to board another plane to Atlanta to meet their parents from several southern states.

I had brought along a stroller and our Alexandra was placed in it. She was watching all the commotion, as Alex from Buffalo, met his new parents and relatives. I was standing in front of her when she looked up and said with a question, "My Mama, my Papa?" I told her we were her Mama and Papa. I handed her a small, white teddy bear. After what seemed like an hour, but in reality was probably five to ten minutes, the adults in the group said it was time for us to leave, to do it quickly, and to expect a loud reaction from our child. As we started pushing Alexandra down the hall to the exit, she began screaming, yelling, and climbed out of the stroller. We had all we could do to hold on to her. I pushed the empty stroller as my husband carried the kicking, screaming Alex to the exit. It is a wonder the airport police did not come after us and think we were kidnapping a child. We hurried along the long distance from the airport terminal to the parking lot as Alex continued to scream, kick, and yell. We placed her in the rear of the station wagon and within five minutes, she was sound asleep.

# 2

## HOMEWARD BOUND

It was about an eight-hour trip from our home to New York. Leaving New York City behind, driving leisurely through New Jersey, Pennsylvania, and across the southern tier of New York State, we had been homeward bound for about four hours when Alex awoke.

We stopped at a rest area, changed her soiled clothes and then found a restaurant to get some food. My husband and I took turns going into the restaurant and brought out food and drink for Alex and us, remembering directions from the agency, saying not to expose them to too much, too soon. After eating and drinking, she wanted to sit up front. I was driving, so she sat on my husband's lap and started playing with the radio. She was babbling in Russian about the lights on the dashboard. She was wide-awake and kept noticing the lights of the towns in the distance fly by and talked about them in her Russian language.

When we arrived home, it was one or two in the morning. Alex's eyes were bright and shiny while ours were tired from the stress of the long trip. At our house, she saw a cat and dog for the first time. In the living room, at one end, was a play area, with a child's table and chairs, books, crayons, games, and other toys. When she saw these, she had to try everything out and it was difficult to get this wide-awake girl to go upstairs to bed.

Her bedroom was waiting across the hall from ours. I let her see her room after she put on a new nightgown. I thought I had her all settled in her bed for the night and proceeded to be settled in my own bed. She had a different idea. Soon she was crying and came into our room and climbed into our bed with us. We let her stay and she slept until morning.

I could imagine how lonely and maybe scared, she had to be. She was in a strange country, in a strange house, in a strange bed, with strange people she had never met before. In the orphanage, she was always with a group of children for everything. Now she was the only one.

However, it did not take Alex long to adjust to all the changes in her life. Because she was not used to animals, she thought the dog and cat were her playmates. She would sit on them, ride them, and pull them around the house. We had to teach her to be gentle with them, even if the cat was almost as big as she was. Both the cat and dog were very good with her, even when she cut the cat's whiskers and the dog's hair. They were, "My Rusty, My Brigette." Our son, she called, "My Joseph." Everything she saw, she called, "My Ma Ma,

my Pa Pa, my house, my
car, etc." as she quickly
learned      the      English
language.

## ADJUSTING

Whenever I was in the
kitchen preparing a meal,
Alex would sit in her high
chair at the table. She
would sing Russian nurs-
ery rhymes, over and over,
and many times would
bang her fist or a fork on
the table indicating she
wanted her food. I learned

this was a common occurrence in the orphanage as the children sat for a long time waiting for food to come in from the
countryside and be prepared. The most common food was a
soup of cabbage, potatoes, other vegetables, and any meat
that could be added to the soup. In spite of the scarcity of
food and because she received no junk food loaded with
sugar and salt or harmful additives, she is a very healthy
child.

We were told to learn a few phrases and words in Russian
so communicating would be easier. I had tapes in Russian and
had listened to them before she arrived and knew a few key
phrases. As soon as she arrived, she began talking English
and gave up all her Russian. I did too. After three months, she
spoke almost perfect English and began correcting my husband's pronunciation of certain words with his German ac-
cent. She would say, "That's not the way to say that word,
Daddy. You should say…" I was her security blanket. She always wanted to know where I was and wanted me to be with

her at all times. If she did not see me or know where I was she would yell, "My MaMa?" Saturday, August 1, 1992, the first day at her new home, I took her to Ames department store to buy her some sneakers, socks and underwear. We stopped at my friend Linda's where Alex received two books and a doll from Linda. Linda became a close ally through the years of raising Alex as well as a welcome influence on her in many ways.

The second day home was Sunday, so while I went to Church, my husband gave Alex her breakfast, or I should say tried to give her breakfast. She looked out the door and noticed that my car was gone. She cried "My Mama! My Mama!" until I returned. Later in the day, my mother, my sister, and my friend, Sandy, came to meet Alex.

On August 29, Alex was baptized in St. Joseph's Church in Albion. It was my husband's 60th birthday. Afterwards we had a big party. Marliese, my husband's sister, came from Germany to visit. She made a big fuss about Alex, holding her and dancing with her at the party. Of course, everyone brought her gifts. Alex loved the attention as well as all the gifts; especially a beautiful flowered dress from Anne and Rita (two of my friends). Some of my former co-workers gave her a shower at our house a few weeks later, which meant lots of toys, books, dolls, and a big red wagon. She was already becoming a spoiled little girl.

## GETTING MEDICAL HELP

She had to get a physical exam by a pediatrician and this was the beginning of correcting her leg problem. Dr. Sahukar thought she might have dislocated hips, so I took her to see Dr. Landfried, who had met her only on video, before her arrival. Now, she was in his office. The x-rays showed she did not have dislocated hips. The possibility of a dislocated hip was so, so unbelievably ironic to me. I, myself, had been born with what was called a dislocated hip... no ball and socket in my left hip... just bone to bone. Luckily, she did not have this problem. This deformity had never stopped me from doing normal things as I grew, but I was greatly relieved that she would not have to deal with this problem, in addition to her mild CP.

The days flew by, as there were many blood tests and appointments and much searching to decide what we would do about her legs and feet. She went just about everywhere I had to go. We visited a friend who had baby pigs and chickens. Another had baby kittens. I took her to my office at Genesee College. Linda took her to Blissett's Children's Store for a new dress and slip. I tried to leave her at my mother's house, but she would not stay without crying "My Mama, Mama, Mama!" After a month, she did not mind staying for a short time. She kept improving and adjusting well to all the new people, places, and things in her life. I noted that after just one week she did the following:

- Takes out one toy at a time and puts it back when finished with it.

- Counts to five on her fingers in English.

- Says her name after I say it.

- Throws waste paper in waste basket.

- Holds dust pan while I sweep.

- Uses her napkin.

- Places things in correct spot, if out of order.

- Is outgoing, very friendly, verbal, makes funny faces.

- Loves the cat, teases the dog. Is afraid of dog, pounds the cat.

- Set the table as I gave her each piece and told her whom it was for, in the correct spot.

- Loves to eat anything. Watches us if a food is new to her, to see if she should hold it in her hands or use a fork or spoon.

- Won't let Mama out of her sight.

- Sleeps all night since first night. (9:00 PM to 7:00 AM)

- Uses bathroom on her own. Wipes.

- Asks for a bath every evening.

- Seems to understand most English commands.

On Saturday, August 8, I had an appointment to get my haircut. Alex had been in America one week. My friend, Linda, said I should leave Alex at her house while I went. Alex cried for Mama for the 45 minutes I was gone. She stood in the window and watched for my car to come down the street.

After Church on Sunday, we went to the Apollo Restaurant for breakfast. Later at home, we were looking at our passports. First, I showed her passport to her; then I showed her my passport; then my husband's. She then asked where our son, Joe's was: "My Joseph?" Looking at photos and the video from Russia, she named the Russian people in them. This amazed all of us.

By six weeks, Alex was learning two new words a day and starting to talk in longer phrases. On September 17, she used a complete sentence in English, having been here one and a half months.

By ten weeks, she did not sing Russian songs any more. She was speaking almost entirely in English. "I don't want to." "What are you doing?" Runs from nursery school teachers, talks back to teachers and parents. She had to sit in "Time Out" for not obeying. "I don't want to" and "I'll throw this dumb paper away" got her in trouble.

# 3

## THE MEDICAL JOURNEY

As I mentioned before, Dr. Langfried, an orthopedic surgeon, had seen Alex prior to our visit to his office, on the video, sent to me by the adoption agency. He and his wife had viewed it and now Alex was in his office. Upon examining her, he made some observations:

1. She is the worst she will ever be.

2. She is very functional for her age.

3. Her mild cerebral palsy was caused by birth trauma (interrupted blood supply to the brain). It is not progressive. Her feet and legs are normal.

4. Mild cerebral palsy in Alex means her lower extremities were affected by a specific part of the brain, which controls leg muscles and cords.

5. Recommended corrections would be: Lengthen hip and heel cords, minor surgery, casts and braces.

Shriner's Hospital in Erie, PA was again suggested.

An appointment was made at Shriner's Hospital. My friend, Sandy, made the 3 hour trip with us. After their examination of Alex, I was told she could be put on a waiting list... it might be a year or more before they could help... the reason being that they deal with much more severe cases... which get serviced first. One young intern said she could wait until she was seventeen and see if anything could be done. This was a big disappointment for me. I could feel my heart tightening up... with feelings of both hopelessness and anger. Walking to the car in silence, asking for divine guidance, I mulled over and over in my mind what I should do and finally as we reached my car, I said, determinably, to Sandy: "I am NOT waiting a year or until she is seventeen." Sandy agreed.

The next stop on the medical journey was the Children's Hospital in Buffalo. We saw Dr. Robert Gillespie, an orthopedic surgeon. He explained that he could operate on Alex's heel cords by inserting a corkscrew type instrument and stretching the cords. She would wear casts to her knees for a month and then braces. Alex told everyone she saw: "Doctor going to cut my feet here, so I walk like this and no more fall down." Her first operation was on November 23, 1992. She had to be carried for 4 weeks with the plaster casts. Then she had two sets of fiberglass casts on which she could walk. On January 8, 1993, she received her thin plastic braces which she wore inside her sneakers. Her right leg was done a second time in 1994. Her hamstrings were done when she was eleven years old, as the teenage growth spurt was making her legs hurt and she was bending forward and walking more awkwardly. While she recuperated, she could not attend school so during this time, I tutored her at home. Visits for follow-up to Dr. Gillespie were always something Alex looked forward to. Dr. Gillespie was very kind and gentle and Alex loved him. When he passed away at age 66 with cancer, she was very sad. She wanted to go to his funeral service so we attended at the St. Joseph's chapel at the University of Buffalo. His work with children involved sending outgrown braces from America to hospitals in Poland, as well as teaching his skills to interns from Europe. As a teenager, Alex later told me that Dr. Gillespie was who she wanted to be like and that she knew she wanted to be in health care... maybe a doctor.

## GROWING AND LEARNING

Two weeks before Christmas a friend dressed up as Santa and came to our house. Even though she had heard about Santa in Preschool, talked about him, and wanted to see him, when suddenly he was there in person, she could not handle it. She screamed, cried, and told him to get out of her house. That evening she told her father to be sure, he locked all the doors so Santa could not get in. However, on Christmas morning she changed her mind about liking Santa. Her favorite gift was a tape recorder. She loved music. Her language developed rapidly and she was able to transfer words and phrases correctly. She would often leave her crayons and toys where the dog could grab them. Talking to the dog, she would ask, "Rusty, why you eat my crayons and my doll?"

During these growing years, she played soccer one summer and became an excellent swimmer. The lifeguards at Faun Lake, where we had a summer place, took special interest in her and spent a lot of time coaching her. Later she had lessons at a private pool. She continued to grow and graduated from tricycles to various sized bicycles.

For the four years in the orphanage, she could not walk, let alone run. She rarely went outside. She usually sat and watched all the others, observing every minute detail of all the interactions. This had to be very frustrating... not being able to run and play like everyone else. Nothing would have been done to correct Alex's problem; no physical therapy. There was no mental stimulation either, as school did not begin until age seven. If she had remained in an orphanage setting, she would have become a handicapped misfit. No wonder she ran everywhere, especially in the halls at school. Often she would knock other kids over because of her awkwardness and imbalance. The teachers had their work cut out for them.

Alex was very healthy... hardly ever sick. Even though the children in the orphanage had meager meals of mostly watered-down vegetable soup with meat added when available, their immune systems were strong from not being exposed to artificial additives, and sugar. In addition, no antibiotics were administered for minor infections. One of Alex's first records from Russia, states that she had her tonsils removed without an anesthetic. I was never able to confirm this.

From the beginning, we could tell that Alex had good verbal skills and a keen ear for music. While listening to a song on the radio, which she had never heard before, she could sing along and match all of the notes with perfect pitch. At age 10, she began piano lessons. Two years of not practicing and not progressing, led to trying the trumpet and then the clarinet. Again, there was no commitment and no desire to practice. Then at 14, she wanted a keyboard for Christmas. She took piano lessons for another year and again, no interest. Singing in the school chorus, then a small group of youth at church, seemed to satisfy her musical gift. At age 15, she became the youngest member of the adult choir of St. Joseph's Church.

Through the Albion Central School District's Committee on Special Education, Alex was evaluated and received physical therapy from Kindergarten through 8th grade. She was totally declassified by 9th grade. On April 10, 2001, Alex had her final checkup at Children's Hospital. Dr. Gillespie was impressed with how far she had come. He said she would always have some problem with her gait, (I have always had trouble with mine all my life), but was not concerned about her right leg being shorter (my left leg has always been shorter than my right, requiring a lift) and her right foot crossing over slightly to the left. He emphasized repeatedly, that the one thing that is necessary, is for her to have a stretching program and to do the exercises as many times as possible. "One hundred times a day is not too much."

I had been searching for a way to help her to be more graceful with her walking and running. I considered videotaping her and letting her friends work with her or remind her to walk correctly with heels down first. She told me she was fine and did not need any help.

Alexandra continued physical therapy for thirty minutes, twice weekly, for a program of stretching, strengthening exercise and gross motor activities. A report on her progress in April of 1999, states: "She is energetic and cooperative in therapy. Despite Alex's limitations, she functions well. She is able to ascend and descend stairs, kicks a ball, and enjoys participating in sport activities."

Soon Alex knew everyone and everyone knew Alex; not only the individuals, but also the names of their friends and relatives. Everywhere we went, she talked to people she knew and I did not. She had become a social butterfly... in school, in church, in the town.

Alex loved her big brother. Joseph built huge snow castles with tunnels for her to crawl in and pulled her on a toboggan behind his four-wheeler across the fields. Easter was as great a thrill as Christmas. Joseph would hide eggs around our yard and she would collect them in her basket. She would often get temporarily upset if she could not go with Joe and his friends. Joe recalls Alex telling him that she was going to marry him when she grew up... a typical expression of love any little girl has for a big brother she adores. She was distressed when he became engaged.

Halloween was frightening at first, but she liked dressing up as one of the three little pigs. On a trip to Letchworth State Park, Alex loved collecting the many colored leaves, which we put in a see-through notebook. She took it to school for "show and tell."

Alex loved books and stories. One day, after reading a library book with her, she kept putting her hand between the book jacket and the book. I told her to stop so she would not hurt the book. She looked at me and asked, "Will the book yell 'ouch?'" Then she laughed and laughed at her play on word meanings.

She loved staying at Faun Lake (our summer get-a-way) three or four days at a time where she would build sandcastles and swim in the pool. Again, she made friends quickly and was at ease talking with strangers upon first meeting them. On the Fourth of July, she was amazed at her first glimpse of a fireworks display.

Sometimes, Alex became a discipline problem; usually by talking back or refusing to do something. If she were told NOT to do a certain thing, she would find a way to do it. When she was five, on her own, she took a screwdriver from her brother's room to her bedroom, removed the screw on the

wall light switch plate, lost the screw, found another (which was the wrong size), and tried to replace it.

Alex loves ice cream. For a while, her favorite was vanilla, and then she switched to strawberry because it was "pink." She went through part of a year where everything had to be pink... ribbons, playhouse, bike, clothes, etc.—A typical phase for any little girl.

Whatever we were doing, she was in the center of it. She "helped" her father pick raspberries, cherries, and currants and sometimes "hoed" the garden. She also liked to wash dishes, sweep the floor, and vacuum. All these chores she did willingly until she was about seven years old, then she refused to follow through on any of them. She liked to rake leaves and hide in them. It was great fun for her to ride on the wagonload of pumpkins at harvest time.

One day, while watching a video about an orphan, Alex burst into tears and sobbing, saying, "I miss my friends in

Russia... Why didn't you get 2 or 3 more kids?" Every few days she would ask if I would get her a brother or sister. At this point, I wished I had been motivated to get more children when I was younger, but the responsibilities of my work and household kept me very busy. Alex continued to bug me with, "I wouldn't have to bother you so much and I would have someone to play with and talk with for the rest of my life." What a super-sensitive, alert little person she was becoming.

During the first year with us, she constantly told us she would take us to Russia to meet her friends. I tentatively planned in my mind to take her back to visit Russia when she was about ten, but circumstances did not allow. I would have been able to research her family through an interpreter and, hopefully, she would learn more about her origin, which she had a great desire to know. Even though I was not able to take her back to Russia, Alex was able to return for 7 weeks in the summer of 2009 with a student group from college.

Being verbal, Alex developed the habit of interrupting adult conversations. At one supper table, Mom and Dad were discussing the stormy weather. I decided I should cancel the afternoon workshop scheduled for the next day. Alex leaned over and said, "That was a good thing to do, Ma Ma." At another meal, Mom passed Dad the salad. Alex said, "Daddy, you could have reached the salad yourself." Dad replied, "Mom is just being nice by passing it."

I took Alex and her friend, Wendy, to Toronto to a theatre to see the play, "Lion King." For a year afterwards, we had a collection of "Lion King" items. Her favorite TV program became Wild America, soaking up all the facts and names of different species of sharks and other animals. Collections of bugs, caterpillars, beetles, and worms often found their way to her bedroom.

Alex became a U.S. Citizen on December 11, 1993 at a special ceremony in Niagara Falls, New York. Alex was one of 44 others who received citizenship from the U.S. Immigration & Naturalization Service. The ceremony was planned around the annual Festival of Lights where the whole city is lit up for the holiday season.

At five years old, she had an extensive vocabulary. When she found a fly flapping around on the windowsill in the sunshine, she asked her father why it was acting like that. He said it had been sleeping. She then said, "You mean hibernating, like the bears and chipmunks do?"... She had an uncanny ability to make associations.

Alex liked to watch football games on TV with her big brother when he was home from college, but she could not keep quiet. They would argue and he would shut her out of the den.

At one point when she was six, she asked for a real toolbox because she wanted to build things as her brother did. We found 4-inch nails pounded into the wooden stairs in the garage. Apparently, Alex wanted to prove to us that she could handle a hammer, or do what Joe did.

Alex received her First Holy Communion in St. Joseph's Church on May 4, 1997. Through her growing years, Alex enjoyed family trips. We visited Germany and Switzerland in 1998 (where Alex met her father's family for the first time) and again in 2002. There was Disneyland in Florida with a family friend, Karen Spierdowis, a teacher. For her 16th birthday, she and I toured New York City.

During Easter break in 2001, when she was 13 years old, Alex and I flew to Washington, D. C. This would be a great age to see and learn about our nation's heritage. The first evening there, I received a call that my husband was in the hospital and needed a brain operation for a subdural-hematoma from an old injury. Many phone calls ensued to try to get transportation home, keep in touch with the doctors, family, and pastor. The next morning, the first day of our tour, I stayed near the bus and made connections on my cell phone, while Alex was able to go with the tour group to most of the sites of D.C. We were able to get the last two seats on a plane to Buffalo and arrived after midnight. The next morning in Rochester, everything went well with the operation.

While a senior in high school, Alex attended Urban Challenge 2006 in Camden, New Jersey. The group of students tore down walls in houses being renovated and made side trips. Alex writes: "We went to Inglis House in Philadelphia, a wheelchair community providing long-term nursing care for 295 residents, adult day-care for people with physical disabilities. We worked in pairs; taking residents to their therapy sessions and meals. I had volunteered in a nursing home for service credit when I was beginning high school and I realized that just being there, even the smallest thing I said mattered to them. Much of my insight has come from scripture... serving the least of God's people. It is a constant reminder of how we are called to serve each other as God looks after us. I am reminded that at any time I may need this assistance and that we are all vulnerable. The strength and determination of the residents allowed me to see God. I definitely learned to be more thankful despite my life circumstances." While in elementary school, she had a part in "Joseph and the Amazing Technicolor Coat" and in high school she was in, "Bye, Bye, Birdie," enabling her to grow in relationships and expand her creative talents.

My Hero . . . . .
He fixed my legs

and I became interested in a _medical_ career.

Alex

# 4

## NOT ALL FUN AND GAMES

In elementary school, she grew academically and usually received glowing reports from her teachers about her positive qualities, however, we, at home, saw a different side of Alex's personality manifesting itself. She would often revert to throwing tantrums as a means to get her own way. She continued to yell, scream, stomp, and cry when she was told "no" to anything. In 3rd grade, I took her to a child psychiatrist who determined that her behavior had a name: "Post-Separation Disorder." Babies are born with a need to attach and bond as they have their needs met. If nobody answers these needs, the cycle of trust is broken. In addition, normal parenting does not work; often resulting in aggression, disrespect, and emotional outbursts.

Most of her defiant behavior was aimed at me, her mother. Doing dishes became the battlefield. "I don't have time to do the dishes. I'll spray them in the sink, instead of putting them into the washer. Okay, (yelling) I'll put them in the washer so you don't have a sissy fit." I was keeping a journal and began to write. "You're going to write this down--Woo, Woo, now write that down too." I reminded her to turn the dishwasher on as she exited the kitchen. She said, "You have to have everything your way, don't you?" Then she stood in the doorway, arms crossed, mumbling that I was a dictator.

Most children can be dealt with by taking items and their favorite activities away for a period, and most will grow out of this misbehavior. Children with Separation Anxiety lasting into the teen years are at a higher risk of developing phobias (afraid of being left alone, an unrealistic worry that something bad will happen to the caregiver or parent, and repeated temper tantrums). Once Alex wrote in one of her papers that her greatest fear was that, I would die before she is grown and able to take care of herself. Even though she could write about these feelings, she continued to have outbursts, usually when she could not have her own way or when she was angry.

In December of 2003, one week before Christmas, Alex decided she would go to the Christmas Dance; until now, she definitely was not going. She would need a new long dress, shoes, and a camera to take pictures because she was the class photographer. I had leg and back pain at this time, and did very little walking. Since she needed a long dress, I took her to the local consignment shop because I had heard they had a good selection. She came out and said they did not have any. Later, I found out there were many. Because I was having a difficult time walking, I would sit in the car while she looked in "Fashion Bug" in Medina. She would not go in by herself and insisted that I go in. Therefore, cane in hand, I managed with great effort to get into the store. Instead of looking at the long dresses, Alex wandered around the store looking at jeans and tops. Finally, I got her to try on three dresses and she picked one. I was in much pain from standing, waiting for her to decide on which dress. It was a relief to get to the car and sit. In the car, Alex said I had to take her to Rochester (30 miles away) to buy a camera. She had forty dollars from her father for Christmas for a camera, so I drove to a nearby drug store and told her to get one in there. She threw a fit that the cameras were junk in drug stores. I told her I could not drive to Rochester even if I wanted to because I was in pain and that she had to buy one here. She refused to get out of the car and go in by herself. I finally got out of the car with my cane and went into the store. She came in behind me, stomping around, saw a camera in the glass case for ninety-five dollars and wanted it because it had an automatic zoom lens. I told her to buy the one with the manual zoom lens for forty-two dollars. She continued her tirade about it being a piece of junk and criticizing me for not taking her to Rochester. She sat in the back seat and started to unwrap the camera package. I told her to wait until she was home and could read the directions. Two minutes later, a flash went off. She had the film and batteries in the camera.

She was able to go to the dance with her dress, shoes, and camera. After the dance, she mentioned that the number of the pictures stayed at "0", so she does not know how many pictures are left... and therefore, proving it is a piece of junk. On Christmas, she was going to finish the roll of film and mentioned again that the number did not advance. Both my sister and I told her it was because the film was not hooked in place to be turned correctly and she probably lost all the pictures. She was furious!

We had company for dinner. We were clearing the table. I asked Alex to give us a hand. Her response was, "You have lots of help; let them do it." My sister told her to get going and help. After much grumbling, Alex sarcastically started in. "Yeah, can you believe she (I) wouldn't go shopping with me? She wanted to sit in the car. She doesn't really hurt... it's all made up."

After what I had endured to get her, at the last minute, what she needed so she could go to the dance, I felt tears starting to fall from my eyes. Hurting, I turned to leave the room before I said or did something I would be sorry for. Alex saw that I was wounded, but she lashed out again, "Look at her, pretending she is in pain; all made up." My sister came to my defense and asked her how she could even think about being a nurse when she had no compassion for her mother, who does everything for her and gets her everything she needs? Alex's reply was that I was "turning on the tears to get sympathy."

Her birthday weekend arrived in February. Two friends from school stayed over-night on Friday. On Saturday, I took them to a movie in Rochester and out to eat. On Sunday, my sister, Joyce, and Wendy (Alex's friend) were here for dinner. My husband and my sister were laughing and joking about something as Alex walked between them. She stopped, looked at her father and said, "Idiot." I jumped up, grabbed her arm and told her we do not call anyone "idiot", especially your father or mother. Her father did not hear what she had said and left the room. Joyce and I tried to talk with her, but she kept up her defense that we were stupid and she did not get enough for her birthday. "Other kids get more. We are technologically decrepit." We do not have all the latest electronic equipment and gadgets for many reasons, but we have enough.

Same year; March 31. Alex planned April fool's jokes with her friends. They were trying to get good ones on certain people… to the point of being mean. I decided I would get one on her. On April 1, Alex came home from school; flopped in front of the TV. I told her I had a big surprise for her. "What is it?" she wanted to know. I told her that on Sept 1 we were getting another girl from Russia. She starting yelling, "How could you do this to me? Are you crazy? I don't want another kid here!" Big tears were rolling down her cheeks as she said repeatedly she did not want another kid in our house. I reminded her of earlier years when she begged me to get her a brother or sister. Finally, she asked if it was a joke and I asked her why she was so upset… that she should want to share her home with someone her age. At supper, she admitted she did not want to share me… my time, energy, money, or attention with anyone else. She wanted to be the only one. Conversation about selfishness did not seem to make a dent and she was angry that I had played an April fool's joke on her.

Friday. April 2: My husband and I told Alex we were going out for a fish fry. She started complaining that she was not going; that she wasn't hungry… why couldn't she stay home and fix something herself to eat. Usually she came to the table complaining we have the same thing all the time… "why can't we eat out?" By now, she was yelling that she would not go. We say, "Okay, stay home. We are going." She yells to wait for her to change her clothes and put on her shoes. We told her we are not waiting. We left. When we came home, she had locked us out of the house and would not answer our knocking. She stayed in her bedroom at the other end of the house all evening. This was yet another example of trying to show us that she was in charge and calling the shots.

Patience, patience! Love is patient. Nevertheless, at times, all the nurturing, care giving, and reassuring, did not seem to be enough and I had to admit that all my 34 years experience of working with children was put to the test, as Alex's defiant behavior was very annoying and frustrating. She was more of a challenge than all my foster children and problem students taken as a whole group in 34 years.

Another anxious time was when Alex was about 7 years old. She wanted to go sledding on a Sunday in winter, so my husband put our toboggan in the truck and took her to the local park. I visited my mother and joined them later. At the park, Alex decided she did not like the toboggan and wanted a saucer sled like someone else had. She started her whining.

My husband did not know what to do, so he drove to a nearby store to see if he could buy one.

None was available so they returned to the park to wait for me. She continued her tantrum as her father put her in the truck. As he got in, she picked up an aerosol spray can of de-icer and pointed it at him. He grabbed her hand until she released it. Someone nearby had seen the scuffle and heard her yelling and screaming and had called the police to report child abuse. Meanwhile, I arrived and we headed home. The phone rang and we had to go to the police station. After explaining the situation and talking to Alex, the case was closed. Very embarrassing!

It was times like this that the only answer was prayer. Alex came into our lives for a higher reason. Our children will make decisions, do things and act in ways we cannot comprehend or approve of. We grow as much or more than they do, as we work through these exasperating times and as we weather the storms, our hearts become stronger, more thankful, and patience does grow. Believing in the innate goodness of everyone, we continue to give from our heart. My prayer of thanks would be: Lord, thanks for the blessings of my life. Thank you for this child. Help me grow in wisdom, help my faith to deepen. Give me patience.

# 5

## THE TEEN YEARS ARRIVE

Alex had a dream of riding in a hot air balloon over the Swiss Alps. She said: "As a child my mother took me to a balloon show and I fell in love with them. I choose the Swiss Alps because when I went to Switzerland and was able to climb the mountains, it was so beautiful."

Even in fourth grade, Alex was a computer whiz. She was allowed to help all the other students with their learning and using computers. It was in 4th grade where she developed her excellent writing skills. Her teacher, Mrs. Bannister, took much interest in Alex's creative abilities and inspired her to keep a journal. Reading and writing became a passion, which greatly increased and improved her academics through high school and into college. She writes that her other life goals include getting married and having a big family. In her junior year, she writes about her family: "I think my family is unique with all the backgrounds we represent. My father was a German immigrant, I am Russian, and my mother is English, Irish, and German. They have tried to instill their values of honesty, hard work, and good behavior on me, so I can have a successful life as they have. Another unique aspect is the big generation gap between them and me; mainly, because they are much older than most of the parents of my friends. I was adopted after they had retired from their jobs. I have learned a lot from them and hopefully, I will use them as an example of how to live my life."

Technology can be both a good and a bad thing. It can keep us connected, but it can also isolate us, preventing real relationships to flourish. At the beginning of high school, assignments required more and more time on the computer for facts and research into different topics. A rule in our house was that Alex could use my computer for class work, but the Internet and Instant Messenger were off limits. There were many girl friends, where usually there were three girls trying to outdo or outshine each other. Some names that come to mind are Shayna, Liz, Nikki, Maria, Caitlin, Amber, Jamie, Heather, LeAnn, and Talisa.

Alex found out that Talisa and she had things in common other than a crush on Jared. Both Talisa's parents and we did not allow use of unsupervised computer work and Instant Messenger. Alex told Talisa she figured out a way to get my password, have Instant Messenger installed on Talisa's computer in a way to hide it, and how to delete internet files and cookies. Then they could talk to Jared. Talisa's mother found out and that put a damper on their relationship. A problem with passing notes at school followed. This was not the first encounter with Alex and computer problems. In her own words, she tells of a prior incident:

"I got into trouble in 8th grade for going on the computer too much. My Mom locked the computer room. I found the key and would sneak on about 2:00 am. One night, after coming home from baby-sitting, I went in the chat rooms and talked to my friends. My Mom caught me and from then on things went downhill for me in regards to my parents trust in me. My Mom took the computer to a person who took it apart to see what I had been doing. I was talking to people from other states in the chat rooms. My Mom was very upset, especially when she heard that I had been talking with at least 70 people from all over. One of the "boys" had arranged to meet me at the Library in town. She sent me to a counselor who interrogated me about why I intentionally defied my parents. Then my mother took me to the police youth officer where he informed me that using the computer was a privilege, not a right, and if I should ever do something like this again I could be sent to a program for juvenile delinquents. In addition, he emphasized that, just as I could say I was anyone, the other person could do the same… that I do not know who I am talking to and it can only lead to trouble. Ever since, this whole fallout with my parents, the computer has been a very touchy subject for both my parents and me."

Changes took place in Alex's teen relationships… new boyfriends, more notes with made up messages and gossip, and pranks.

Alex continues: "I played an April Fool's joke on Talisa. I lied when I told her my Mom had found all our notes, that she caught me on the computer and had removed everything from my room; also that the police were sending me to boot camp in the summer; basically that I was in trouble over my head. Looking back on it now I regret doing this and I do not know why I did it. Talisa believed it until I told her it was a joke. This caused her to freak out. She questioned me about the way I acted toward my parents. After this, Talisa and I grew apart. I was just looking for approval. I have a fear of not being what others want me to be and a greater fear of being alone. I think this fear stems from the fact that my birth-mother did not want me and when I was born, she gave me up without even looking at me. But time is passing, and I seem to be getting better with relationships."

There were boyfriends. Anthony was an adopted son of Alex's first physical therapist. They shared the same age and a love of music. Anthony was very gifted and was a member of the Eastman School of Music Children's Chorus. Alex was fortunate to go with his family to some of the performances. In her Senior Class Assessment, she writes extensively about Drew, calling the section, "My Green Light." The green light reference is regarding the relationships in "The Great Gatsby," read in English class.

Our friendship began in Fourth grade in September of 1998. We were inseparable, sitting next to each other at lunch, during class, playing and chasing each other on the playground. In fourth grade, I had to wear braces on my legs to help me walk better. All the other guys made fun of me, but not Drew. Even at ten years old I felt comfortable when around him and never had to feel that I had to act differently. I could tell him anything and he would listen. He was upset when my parents sent me to St. Mary's School in Batavia starting in fifth grade. I remember when I had surgery and had to wear casts that went from my thighs to the tip of my toes for about two months. Since I could not go to school, my Mom taught me at home. I remember one day when Drew and his mother came to visit me. He brought me a beanie baby present, signed my cast, and we played card games.

In 2000, Drew's family adopted a little six-year old boy, Sam, from Russia. Drew's mother told me later that the one reason why they adopted from Russia was because I was also from Russia. At first, Drew did not like the idea of having a little brother since he had been an only child all his life. I became Sammy's babysitter. for three years. I am thankful for the experience because I got to see Drew often. We talked about our plans, and college. His grandparents had a cottage at Lake Ontario, about three miles from my home, where he and his parents spent a lot of time in the summer. I was invited there to swim, fish, and go tubing in the lake. We went to "Brown's Berry Patch" for subs and ice cream. He also came to my house where we would watch movies and play games. I was happy to talk with him, liked him a lot, and always had his latest school picture in a frame on my night stand.

Junior Prom time arrived. I was at Notre Dame and Drew was at Albion High School. Ever since I started going to school dances, my Mom would always mention that I should ask Drew to a dance. I said "no" because I had heard he never went to dances, but I really wanted to ask him and had been thinking about it a lot. When I finally asked him he replied, 'Wow, I am flattered. I would love to go with you.' It took about three weeks to find out if he could go or not, because three days after I asked him, he went off to Germany and India for Easter vacation. During this time, I started thinking seriously about him. I would think about great elaborate things that could happen and get myself all psyched up, only to be disappointed. That was not out of the ordinary for me... I would always do that anyway. I was so happy that he would finally be able to meet all my friends and we could hang out and talk. As my Mom said, we were going to be going on our first date! I had a wonderful time at the prom, but it was not what I had imagined in my fantasy. I wanted to tell him how much I would love our friendship to turn into something more, but I did not. From what my mother and others thought, Drew probably, most likely, knew that I liked him. Three weeks after the prom, Drew and I went out to eat after the SAT exam.

I now see that he has changed greatly from when we were younger. We do not share as much in common. He likes to party. Seeing the kind of person he is, does not exactly make me think less of him, but I realize that I am not used to the type of lifestyle he has. Ever since fourth grade, he wanted to go to Georgetown University. We both want to go to medical school. He will be a long way from home and I want to stay closer to home. I am only 17 and have a lot of time ahead of me to think about these things. I would rather both of us go off to college, still be friends, with him knowing how I feel. I have waited seven years: I can wait seven more. I have learned much about myself. All things happen for a reason and I think this relationship has taught me not to hold on to the past as much as I do. I must let go, accept things for what they are, be happy with what I have been given, and move on. I should not let my past desires limit me from bettering myself or getting in the way of my dreams.

## SORTING THINGS OUT WITH MUSIC

As part of their Senior Assessment assignment, students were to prepare a scrapbook of favorite photos, attach a favorite piece of appropriate music to each photo and write why they belong together. I include the major sections here as a record for Alex to look back on for years to come.

A PICTURE OF ME IN NEW YORK CITY: I have just arrived from Russia. The teddy bear I am holding was the first thing given to me by my Mom. Two songs fit this occasion: Celine Dion: "Because You Loved Me" and "A New Day Has Come." It was a new day, a new beginning, in a new land. Thanks to the love and compassion for others that my parents decided to adopt me.

MY FAMILY: My parents, my brother, Joseph, and my Grandmother. My grandmother meant a lot to me. The last two years of her life, she lived with us and I gave up my room for her. Looking back now, I know that she allowed me to learn about older people and to have respect for them. It was at her death that I was fully able to understand what death meant and that it was natural for all people. I do regret that I did not spend more time with her. She most likely knew how I felt.

My mother is the best person I know. The song, "Perfect Fan," by the Backstreet Boys, explains how I feel about her. Everything she has done for me, no matter how small, has meant a lot to me. She, as well as my father, has sacrificed much to get me to where I am. It was my mother who worked at getting me the proper surgery for my legs. I know she will always be there for me. She assured me of that when I was little and was afraid that, because of her older age, she would not be around a long time. My mother has always encouraged me to do things and to step out of my boundaries. Although I have not agreed with everything she has had me do, and gave her much trouble at times, I know she has my best interests at heart. I hope when I have children that I will be as good a mother as she has been to me.

For my father, I use the song, "Butterfly Kisses," by Bob Carlise to represent our relationship. When the song was first released, I had it on my cassette and would go around the house singing it for him. It is about a daughter growing up and the father accepting that fact. I would miss most, my Dad playing his accordion, as well as his frequent lectures about religion.

My brother, Joseph: One day when I was little, I went into my brother's room and this song was playing on his radio: "I Saw the Sign," by Ace of Base. I listened to it with him and liked it very much, so every time I heard it playing I would go into his room and sing, "I saw the Sun." I did it so often he got mad at me. Now every time I am with him and I hear it, we both look at each other and laugh. Joseph is the coolest. We played dominoes and Rummy a lot. Now he lives far away. I miss him a lot.

MY FIRST SURGERY: All I remember is getting up early to drive to the hospital, meeting the doctor before surgery, and walking down the long hallway to the operating room. I was scared, but my doctor, Dr. Gillespie, was a very nice person so I was less scared. When in the operating room, I remember the anesthesiologist putting the mask on me and me trying to pull it off. To calm me they told me jokes about big elephants. After surgery, I remember crying a lot, but having fun with the button you push to dispense your own medication. Mom stayed with me. I believe this experience was what first got me interested in the medical field.

BEGINNING OF FAITH: One of the most important aspects of my life is my faith. Having been brought up in a Catholic household, I cannot see myself without church in my life. My baptism was very painful for me, as well as for the priest. The priest talked slowly and I had to stand (at the time, on my toes: this was before my first surgery), which made me cry. After a while, Mom picked me up and held me for the remainder of the ceremony.

GOING TO GERMANY: In 1998, I met my father's family. He is the oldest of six. Mom, Dad, and I were there for three weeks and got to spend Christmas with them. The first picture is of my cousin, Ulrike. I remember hanging out in her room and playing the Backstreet Boys CD all afternoon and I sang to it. In 2002, my father and I took a trip back to Germany. On this trip I also visited France, Switzerland, Liechtenstein, and Italy.

For my 12th birthday, I got to go to Disneyworld (Feb. 16, 2000) an important event in my life. I went with my Mom's best friend's daughter, Karen. This was because my Mom would not have been able to do all the walking in the parks and she had been there many times before with my brother.

Three wonderful days in Epcot, Animal Kingdom, Magic Kingdom, and MGM.

MANY FRIENDS: With my part in "Bye, Bye Birdie" I made more friends and became more outgoing. Shayna and I became best friends. I choose a lyric from the Ashlee Simpson song, "L.O.V.E." which says, "ups and downs, highs and lows, no matter what, you see me through." Shayna has always been there for me and given me great advice.

'Sophomore Slump' and 'Comeback of the Year' by the Fall Out Boys was on Felicia's CD player. She, Meghan and I would listen to it when we first started Health Careers because we loved their songs. There is a picture of me volunteering at the VA Hospital. I choose the Fall Out Boys song, 'Our Lawyer Made Us Change the Name of This Song So We Wouldn't Get Sued' because Meghan and I love it and it reminds us of each other. I choose the song, 'Photograph,' by Nickelback because it is about looking back at high school and saying goodbye to friends.

My final two songs by Chantel Kreviazuk: 'Time' and 'Weight of the World' represent my feelings about how I have grown up so quickly. I cannot believe I am finally graduating and heading to college. I am ready to spread my wings and fly. I must never forget who and what got me here.

## ALONG CAME KEVIN…WHAT'S HIS NAME?

Senior year, February 24, 2006. Alex's friend Meghan was dating Tim and Tim had a friend named Kevin, so a blind date was arranged. Tim told Kevin there was this girl from Notre Dame he wanted him to meet. The location of the date was Tim's house. Alex remembers taking forever to get ready and finally settling for a pink dress shirt and a zip up light red sweater. It was a clear night with stars visible. My friend, Anne, was visiting for the weekend, so we drove Alex to

Tim's home where Meghan and Kevin were waiting. Kevin came out to the car to meet Anne and me. They watched "The Simpson's" on TV, and then went to the Rec room in Tim's basement to watch a movie. Tim played Xbox before they watched "Fight Club." Alex tried to play but she could not figure out the controls. Then they sat on the couch and watched the movie, with a big space between them. The movie was confusing and Alex kept asking Kevin what was going on. He did not know either. Tim drove Alex home. Kevin and Alex rode in the back seat. They talked about the music they liked. Alex found out Kevin only listened to video game music and immediately told him she would have to enlighten him about music. At our house, Kevin came inside for a moment. Alex was nervous and did not introduce Kevin, so I asked Alex, "What's his name?" She replied something like, "Uhhhh, I don't remember." So then, Kevin introduced himself. This episode has become a standing joke among us… "What's his name?"

More dates and encounters occurred and their friendship grew. Kevin went to Alex's prom at Notre Dame in May and Alex went to his prom in Elba, in June. In September, they went their separate ways to college.

# 6

---

## WHERE AM I GOING AND WHAT IS MY FUTURE?

In a paper that Alex wrote in high school, she stated: "I have made the decision to become a Physician Assistant and plan on attending Daemen College. I had originally been interested in becoming a doctor, yet, I choose PA because I do not think I could handle all the pressure and responsibility of a doctor. One of my dreams has been to work with premature babies, mainly because I was one myself. I know how lucky I am to be here today. My mother and I have explored alternative medicine for many years and I find it fascinating. Holistic medicine, which incorporates the mind, body, and spirit, may in the future work more closely with traditional medicine, providing even better health care."

Graduation from Notre Dame High School was in June of 2006. Alex had her driving license and worked as a cashier at the Save-A-Lot grocery store part-time. September came and off she went to Daemen College. She lived in an apartment with three other girls. Alex liked the campus because it was small. She was able to come home almost every weekend. She liked her courses, but found the social life not to her liking. She was often alone, in her room studying while the other girls went out partying. They would try to have her join them at fraternity parties at the nearby university, but she did not like that behavior; especially when she saw how they talked and acted upon returning from a night of carousing. She always wanted to get A's, but found her grades were slipping and began to worry about her average. In order to stay in the PA program you had to maintain a B+ average. In the second year, she was scheduled with two science courses in the same semester, along with four other classes. She found it difficult to keep up with all the labs and course work. Her roommates were friendlier this year, but she was homesick and wanted to be closer to her boyfriend, Kevin. She went to a college counselor for depression. After much thought, she changed her major to nursing because she could transfer all her science credits. The cost of college was beginning to drain my savings so instead of sending off a check to the college each semester, I decided it would be wiser to invest the money, so in the summer of 2007, I bought two houses, which were in foreclosure. Both were sold in 2009 at a 10% profit… a good return considering the bad real estate market from 2008 on. The financial effect on my bank account was greatly lightened.

I had broken my right shoulder and arm in the fall of 2007 and this slowed me down and complicated what I could and could not do. Alex became more and more anxious about my health issues. In the spring of 2008, I had to have an aortic valve replacement. I had complications, was in the hospital the month of June, then rehab, then scar tissue removal operations, breathing problems, and finally a trachea in my throat. During this time Alex, decided she wanted to live at home and attend State University at Brockport.

Brockport has an excellent nursing program so she transferred. She says she likes Brockport much better than Daemen because she is home. She is around (sometimes) if I need something (she was worried about my health). Also, she could see Kevin more and work more hours at the store. By changing careers and transferring, she lost a year's time.

At Brockport, she was able to take Russian classes, which she had wanted for a long time. Her Russian teacher, Liza, led a group of students to Russia each summer so Alex signed up for the seven-week program and would earn twelve credits when finished. Now, one of her life goals would be realized: To visit Russia. There was a problem getting her visa because she was the only one of 12 students who had been born in Russia. Finally, it arrived the day before departure, after I had spent hours working through diplomatic channels.

# 7

---

## BACK TO RUSSIA

As I write this section of her story, I choose to use much of Alex's own words from her E-mails to her blogs and me. Before she left, she set up her own blog, A Simple Traveler, and signs them as "Sasha," which is Russian for Alexandra. As usual, Alex leaves much to do at the last moment. The evening before her departure, she and Kevin were in her room. Kevin was helping her put all her records and books on the top shelves of her closet. Her father and I had reminded her throughout the day that she would have to go to bed early so she could get up and be rested for early morning traveling. As 10:00 pm approached, her father told Alex that Kevin had to leave by 10:00 so we could all rest. There was no reply or response from them as they continued to do last minute packing. Finally, my husband went to her room and said Kevin was to leave immediately or there would be trouble. A few tense moments followed. Kevin left and met us at the airport the next morning. Apologies were given and accepted, and Alex was on her way. In her own words:

### GETTING READY TO LEAVE:

So silly, really. Do not get me wrong, I am beyond ecstatic that I am doing this... it's scary and will be the hardest thing I have ever done. Personal goals for me on this trip will be to learn to be more independent, less anxious, less afraid, and more trusting of God and myself. One the best ways to do this is to go to a foreign country without the familiarities of home. My first big hurtle will be the plane ride. Even though I have traveled over the ocean before, I am quite scared of flying.

Today, my last day, I have a bit of cleaning to do in my room, last minute packing, and a quick trip to Brockport to pick up crayons and coloring books to take to the orphanage where I will be doing an internship while in Russia. Mom made meatloaf for dinner and apple pie for desert... some of my favorites. Therefore, for now, I will play my Coldplay music loud, and keep forcing memories of my wonderful summer I have had with my friends to stay with me, and of course, Kevin. I can see myself crying a lot tomorrow at the airport. Then there is Moses (my loving cat), to pet for the last time. Tonight, Mom, Kevin, and I watched the James Bond movie," From Russia with Love." Mom wanted me to watch it to get a feel of Russian culture. There really isn't anything to be learned about Russia from the movie. The only thing Russian was the spy. It was a good movie, even though I was falling asleep. Kevin says there are other Bond movies that are actually set in Russia.

A final note, again, thank you for taking the time to read this, pray for me, and I appreciate everyone who has helped me go on this amazing trip. I love you.

## JULY 3, 2009 FIRST DAY IN RUSSIA:

Hello from Russia! I made it safely thankfully. I am writing this at 8:53 pm on Friday. Back where you are its 12:53 pm. Here, the sun is shining brightly and I can tell this is really going to mess up my sleeping. I am tired, but can't bring myself to sleep... it's too bright! It feels strange to be here. I think

I will be home soon, and then I realize I will be here for the next seven weeks.

I was anxious most of the time on the flight to JFK from Rochester. We were late landing. I met the rest of the group and we took AirTrain to our terminal, which reminded me of Frankfurt airport. I hate those moving sidewalk things. I got on one and lost my balance. I was dragging my suitcase, holding my ticket case with my passport and tickets when it flew out of my hand. (I know what you are thinking Mom..."Oh, my, I knew something like this would happen...") It happened so fast, we were moving, and there it was on the other side of the belt. Therefore, Adrian, without even thinking, jumped over the railing like a monkey and retrieved it. After the fact, we all laughed about it. Luckily, there were not a lot of people around and I did not have to worry about anyone stealing it.

Our plane to Helsinki via FinnAir was supposed to leave at 5:40. We were delayed. We took off at 6:55 and at 6:58; the air speed was already 163 mph. The flight time was estimated to be 7 hours and 28 minutes, arriving at 9:27am (Helsinki time... 7 hours ahead of N.Y.). The best part of these flights, in my opinion, is the entertainment systems in the seats... movies, TV, and music. I decided to watch an international film, "Penguins in the Sky." After a dinner of grilled chicken, mushrooms, broccoli, potato patty, salad, roll, and brownie, I watched videos about traveling in Japan and India and listened to some Japanese and Indian Hits on radio. I tried to sleep, then it was time for breakfast... ham and cheese on a sub roll, strawberry/banana yogurt, orange juice and coffee. My legs were really sore and heavy. It was neat that these planes had flight maps so you can watch where you are and tell you how fast the plane is going and how high up you are. The biggest numbers I noticed included 585 mph ground speed, and true airspeed of 546; altitude 39,000 feet.

I was excited to be over Helsinki. Someday I want to visit Sweden or Finland. My sense of adventure was kicking in and I thought, "There is so much of the world to see, if only we didn't have to spend most of our lives working." However, wow, I am beside myself, realizing that I am doing something awesome! The people in the Helsinki airport were laid back, relaxed, not rushing around. They were very polite, had awesome accents and were good looking. I wish things in America were more peaceful and slower paced. We in the group were the ones who had to rush. We finally caught our plane; left at 10:45, instead of 9:30. Helsinki is 300 km from St. Petersburg... so close. We landed at 12:35; the worst landing of the three flights. On another note, watching the clouds from the windows leads me to two different thoughts. They look like they are suspended in air. I want to reach out and touch them, imagine them being soft and being able to jump on them. Over Sweden, they look like ground or the arctic; other places they were really big and fluffy.

The Russian airport, near St. Petersburg, was a lot different from the other two... We went through customs. When we saw our bus, it was a bit comical. The space in the back for luggage was small and we had huge suitcases. Driving in Russia is a nightmare; people are crazy in what they do.

It took two hours to get to Novgorod, our destination and home base. Most of us fell asleep. Driving in this city was even worse with pedestrians all over the place, walking in and out of traffic whenever they pleased. Insane! Anyways, the van (bus) let me out at the bus stop directly in front of Olga's (My host mother's home). She met me with her dog, Beesha. We got to her apartment after lugging my suitcase up four flights of stairs... so glad to be here! Olga also has a cat, Shira. She loves my room and I often find her climbing around my things. She is very entertaining.

First thing I did was take a shower. I have never felt so disgusting in my life. Olga's apartment is small, but I knew this before I came.

Then we ate! Olga is an amazing cook! She made egg and sausage, and a perogie looking thing with dill. All baked, along with lettuce, tomatoes, cucumbers, bread and yogurt on the egg stuff. It was really good. I can tell I am going to like her cooking. Then we had tea. Green tea and chocolate. Normally I do not drink tea at home, but for some reason I did not mind it.

Our communication consists of frequently looking up words in the English/Russian dictionary, along with hand gesture, lots of laughs and patience. Liza, my Russian teacher and tour guide, seemed evil when she sent me off the van with a grin and a push, but the minute I saw Olga, I felt comforted. After tea, I got things in order in my room and Olga and I sat together on the couch and shared photographs and things about our families and us. I found out that Olga was a geography teacher and has traveled to many places including Egypt, Belgium, France, Germany, and New York. At this point Olga went out to walk her dog and go to the store. I got into my PJ's and started writing. Already, I feel so welcome and at home with Olga. This is going to be a great trip!

Our group consists of Liza, Don (who has come to Novgorod many times; this is his fourth; he will help me with Russian). The rest of the group includes Francesca, Michelle, Adrian, Jim, Doug, Steve, Matt, and Magda (from Poland) and me. The last three are not Brockport students. The youngest is eighteen, the shortest is I. Francesca and I are going to make a good team. She does not worry enough; I worry too much, so we balance. Michelle is the "mom." We are like the three musketeers. Then there are the guys! I like the group a lot. Now I must go to bed... Let's see, I've been up almost 32

hours, with only 4 hours of some type of sleep. It's 10:45; the
sun isn't bright now; it's twilight. Tomorrow we are touring
the Kremlin, Sophia Cathedral and Yaroslav Court. Miss you
lots.

## JULY 4TH HAPPY HOLIDAY

I feel comfortable here at Olga's. I woke up at 4:45, stayed
up until 5:35, writing in my journal, then went back to sleep
with my blanket over my head to keep out the light. I woke
up again at 11:10. Olga knocked on my door and told me it
was breakfast time. For breakfast, Olga made omelets with
crème in them. The crème looked like cream cheese, but was
sweet and was the consistency of yogurt. All of this was
called Blini. Apparently, on Russian holidays you eat lots of
blini. I think she made it for us because it was the 4th of July.
We also had green tea.

Olga and I took the bus to the Kremlin where we met the
rest of the group. To get to the Kremlin, I have to take bus 20
and get off at the fifth stop. To return I take bus 19. The bus
makes frequent stops, and there are lots of buses taking people back and forth around the city. I have a bus pass. The
group met, and we figured out how to get back home at night.
Host families were to meet us at 8:00 at the statue of Lenin,
across from the Kremlin. Here we met Colin, from Texas, who
was joining our group only for an internship.

We started our tour with a statue of Sergei Rachmaninov.
Onto the Kremlin, which is about 10 minutes by bus from
Olga's. The word "Kremlin" means "fortress." The Kremlin is
the heart of Novgorod, home of St. Sophia Cathedral, built in
the 11th century. The walls of the Kremlin are brick with nine
towers. Many parts are being renovated now for an 1150 anniversary celebration in September. Putin is coming to
Novgorod in August.

The foundations of the Novgorod Kremlin were laid by Prince Yaroslav the Wise. It is the oldest remaining Kremlin in Russia. It functions as an administrative, civic, and religious center. Alexander Nevsky gathered here before fighting the Swedes. Historical records are kept here and collections of books.

Sophia Cathedral is one of the oldest stone buildings in Russia (1045-1050) and is dedicated to the Holy Wisdom of God. Inside are many religious icons and pretty chandeliers. We were not allowed to take pictures. Magda, Steve, Katya, (the tour girl), and me, decided on a little adventure. There was a door you were not supposed to enter. Magda and Katya wanted to go in really bad so they did, Steve and I where there so we all sneaked in. There was a winding staircase and the girls were ahead of us. They got further ahead when all of sudden we heard a noise as if they fell. They came running down, yelling, "Babushka," which is "grandmother," or "old lady," and they were laughing. Apparently, at the top of the stairs, there was a door where the church choir would sing, and a Babushka was guarding the door and heard them. Babushka never saw us, but it was a thrilling experience running down the stairs. There were Babushkas down stairs too; they just sit in various places and make sure people are behaving. People like us.

One of the five main domes of the cathedral has a dove on top. Legend says that the dove saw all the killing of people by Ivan the 4th as it flew over the church and turned to stone. Novgorod sits on the Volkhov River, which ran red with blood from Ivan's three-day rampage.

On to The Monument to the Millennium of Russia (1862); built by Mikhal Mikeshin. It was the idea of Emperor Alexander, the II. It was placed in Novgorod because Novgorod has a key role in the creation of the Russian State. The monument is divided into three levels: The Church, the Monarchy, and the People. On the top is a figure of an angel blessing a kneeling woman, representing Russia. The second tier has six groups of figures, each representing one of the stages in the development of the Russian State. The statue is round with Peter the Great on the northern side of the monument. The low tier is a complete time line of Russian history. Liza's tour ended here and we were on our own until 8:00. Therefore, we went to the bank, exchanged my American money, and went for pizza. It took us longer to figure out how to split the bill than to eat the pizza. Apparently, the woman who makes it learned how to make it in Italy. We toasted to the 4th of July and enjoyed ourselves. All nine of us ate for around 30 dollars.

The group split up from here. Masha, Doug, Steve, and I decided to walk around the city. We were bench hoping for about two hours because we were so tired. We would walk, find a bench, sit, and walk, find another bench. One bench was at the Victory Memorial. Very pretty! As we walked across the park, we came to an amusement park with blow-up areas and rides for children. Around the park are many roadside stands where you can buy ice cream, popcorn, helium balloons, water, soda, and snacks.

Olga picked me up at 8:00 and took me home in her little red car; the same color as my Mom's car at home. For dinner, Olga made pasta with an Alfredo type sauce, cooked with chucks of ham and dill. For dessert, strawberries with crème and green tea. After dinner, I showed Olga my pictures from today and we watched TV. There was an American movie with Danny DeVito; dubbed with Russian.

I saw a most interesting sight today! While wandering around the Kremlin walls, near the beach of the river, there was a boy being held by his father a few feet above the ground, with his pants down. He was going number two, and his behind was there for the entire world to see.

Another thing, there were three weddings today. The couples were walking around, having their photos taken by the Monument to the Millennium and in front of St. Sophia's. I assume they were getting married in the cathedral.

I see many children, young adults riding bikes, motor bikes, and scooters. One man was rollerblading on what looked like skis with wheels and ski poles. Looked like he was doing laps around the outside of the Kremlin. The city is very beautiful; I enjoy the architecture so much. There is a small park with nice big trees; many places to walk and sit on benches.

It is warm and sunny in the afternoon, but during our adventure, it got cold and rained, but then the sun came out again and it was nice. Olga said the weather in July is cold and rainy... that August is much better.

Today, Olga said she went to her Dacha, (a small shed with a garden plot) to pick strawberries and other vegetables.) Liza had told us that if we had a chance to visit a dacha, to go. I am sure I will have the opportunity to visit Olga's dacha, which is 10 minutes by car from her home.

## SUNDAY, JULY 5TH:

I checked my E-mail today at the Telecom building in the city across from the Kremlin. You have to pay for 30 minutes of computer time. Steve, Masha, and I split the time to send quick messages to our families. Maybe tomorrow we will find a place where wireless is free. Google is in Russian. I have to find out how to switch languages. Yahoo was in English.

Olga made omelet with cooked tomatoes and dill for breakfast. She grows dill at her dacha. After breakfast, I called Michelle and Francesca as we planned to go to a rugby game at the beach and a concert at 2:00, with Elena, daughter of Francesca's host.

Since it was raining, we decided not to go to the rugby game; instead, we took a bus to the other side of the Volkhov River. We went to a department store with four floors. The first floor had a grocery store, watches, a café, washing machines, pianos, and digital cameras. The second floor was filled with kitchen gadgets and house wares. The third floor had music, books, cards, journals, and the fourth floor had kid's toys. I ended up buying a small children's book about Santa, "Father Frost," postcards, an English/Russian phrasebook, and last but not least, a CD of all Coldplay hits: "the Best of Coldplay."

Coldplay is my favorite band. I already have all of theirs, but really was excited about finding this one. It is two CD's of 34 songs. I have never seen it in the U.S. All of this cost me 404 Rubles, which is about 14 dollars. After shopping, I had to find a place to buy more minutes for my cell phone. You put money in an ATM machine, give it your cell phone number and it puts money on your phone. One minute is one Ruble. However, it costs 5 rubles per minute to use.

We came across a Catholic Church where the concert was, but we did not want to pay 30 rubles to go in. I took a picture instead. We decided to get something to eat. The four of us went into a small café. We decided on tea and sausage rolled in a pastry, like a hot dog in a crescent roll. Elena helped us translate. She informed us that blini is something you eat during Russian holiday, when winter turns to spring; like Mardi Gras. Blini are a symbol of the sun (pancakes), and you can put whatever you want in them. We practiced some Russian words. We walked to some more stores. Masha was trying to find a SIM card for her phone. We went to a flower shop and an Adidas store.

While we waited to cross the busy street, a car with a purple joker painted on it, was turning the corner. I tried to take its picture, but I missed. As we crossed the street, the car turned around, stopped for a few seconds, and the driver smiled at Masha and me so I could take the picture... he had realized I wanted his picture. Later on, we saw another car with a large cheetah type cat on it. I am easily amused.

Elena's guy friend, Michael, picked us up at the big department store and took us home... we did not have to ride the bus!

Dinner tonight was good again. Olga made a kind of meat, reminded me of pork chops. We had potatoes with dill and onion, salad with egg and dill and onion and dressing. Olga opened a bottle of red wine. I had a small glass, which made me tired; I was falling asleep. After dinner, I practiced reading aloud the new things I had learned and finished my homework. We had tea and Olga took Beesha for his walk. I read a book, Olga returned, and I went to bed. First day of school tomorrow, have to get up at 7:00. School starts at 9:00. Goodnight. Miss you all!

## FIRST DAY OF CLASS:

Olga made egg, cheese, and a sausage for breakfast. She packed me a lunch, and then we left at 8:00. Instead of taking the bus, Olga and I went by taxi to school, Number 20. The school is located on the opposite side of the river from my house. After we got off at the street the school is located on, we had a 5-minute walk through a little park. I get to school and find everyone.

It starts with Russian Language from 9-12. The teacher is Tamara. The teacher expected us to know more than we did, realizing, she smiled and backtracked a bit. Our textbook cost 500 rubles; not bad compared to prices at home. We did the first few pages in the book... reminding me of a coloring book. Overall, I find that we are at the level of a Russian first grader and if Russia has Are you smarter than a fifth grader? we would all lose. Because I am Russian there is an expectation that the language will come easier to me... not so!

After Russian class, we ate lunch outside. We are not actually at the university and I do not know if this building with many classrooms is connected to the university. Olga's packed lunch was good. I think I had the best-looking sandwich out of everyone! It was two pieces of bread; on each, she put mayonnaise, lunchmeat, cheese, and dill. With it, she packed tomatoes, cucumbers and chocolate cookie bars, and apple juice. I was so happy. I have not had lunch packed for me since grade school. I gave some of my crust to the pigeons. It is so nice that Olga makes sure I get the right bus and gives me lunch. She really cares and that is so reassuring.

Next was Art Class. Our teacher is a locally known artist in Novgorod and she focuses on folk art. She has us working on painting a folk art design on a wooden plate. I have a bad habit of not cleaning off the brush when mixing paint to make new colors. I can see Mom cringing as I ruin her paints or brushes. I also make a mess. Liza said, "Sasha, stop cleaning, wait until you are all finished." She left for a while and when she returned she said, "When I left, Sasha was cleaning; when I return, Sasha is cleaning." This time I was wiping off the table where I missed the edge. Good thing it is water based paint.

Painting ended at 2:00 so we took a bus back to the other side of the river...the one I live on....to a Folk Art Center... This is my favorite part of Novgorod so far. There were tons of people around. Young men were being drafted into the army and their families were there to wish them well and say goodbye. Russian law requires that at age 18 every man serve in the army. A man can get out of it, if he or his family pays a large sum of money (as large as the price of a house).

At the Folk Center, we met in a large room where there were two women dressed in old- fashioned folk Russian dress. We played folk games. Some were silly; others included hot potatoes and variants of it, where you dance in partners or threes. Finally, we had tea and blini with currant jam.

After tea, we were free to go on our own. Stas, the nice man who coordinates a lot of what we do, and Liza's right hand man, wanted to show Francesca and me where we will be doing our internship. The orphanage is a short walk from the Folk Center. Francesca and I start our internship at the orphanage from four to six tomorrow. I am really excited.

Dinner tonight was the most American I have had so far: chicken, mashed potatoes, salad, and tea with chocolate. At tea, Olga and I spend most of the time talking. I ask her where she got Beesha and Shira. Beesha was a gift. Shira was found near the Kremlin; very small, very sick, had medical attention, now she is good. Other than that, Olga asks me what I did during the day and makes sure I use the correct words; we look up the ones I do not know, and vice versa.

Other things I have noticed: Many stray cats. Strangers do not usually smile at each other. Cucumbers here are pear shaped, not long and round, like in America. Women dress very nicely. They wear nice shoes, with high heels. I do not know how they can do that; the roads are very bumpy, lots of potholes and mud puddles. I hear on the news that Obama is coming to Russia. For some reason, that makes me laugh. I took some pictures of where I live.

## FIRST DAY OF INTERNSHIP- THE ORPHANAGE

We had a quiz today in Language class. We will probably have one every day. Oh well. Painting went better. I was not as messy and I cleaned my brushes before mixing colors. I am painting a spoon and a small plate. While we were painting outside there was a radio playing English music, which had been redone in Russian. It seemed so strange, but we enjoyed it.

Classes ended around 2:00, then Francesca and I have our internship from 4-6. Instead of going home and then coming back, today I went to her house. Francesca and I ate vegetables, like a stir-fry that Elena had left over, and then we had tea with something that looked like cookie dough, but tasted like cheesecake with raisins. I also put strawberries on mine. These strawberries are better than in the U.S.; they are smaller, however, they are less watery, sweeter, and taste a whole lot better.

At first, being at the Orphanage I was uncomfortable. Personally, just watching the children was weird, in the sense that, WOW, I used to be one of them! I was thinking so many things, it was crazy. I am anxious to know what kind of circumstances led them here, and I wonder what kind of life they will have... a lot to think about and to take in. I know I am very lucky.

The children were just coming in from outside and it was time to have tea and eat when Francesca and I arrived. They were given small saucers of what looked like soup. Reminded me of the stories Mom told me about me. There are ten children from 4-7; an even number of boys and girls. They are adorable. At first, they could not say anything to us because they had to eat, and then get ready to play outside. They just watched us and we watched them.

The building that they live in is not as big as I thought it would be, but compared to the size of homes and apartments here, it is big. There is a large main room where there are chairs and tables for coloring, a piano, a TV, drawings on the walls, a few couches. Off to the side are three or four rooms on one side and a hallway on the other side that leads to other parts of the building. I assume this is where the kitchen and offices are for the workers.

We went outside and the little girls introduced themselves. They seemed shy, however, that could be because of the language barrier. The workers got some balls; we got in a circle with some of the girls, and tossed the ball around. Eventually this led to practicing Russian and English vocabulary.

One little girl, named Alla, is very interested in the English language and seems overall very smart and quick at learning. She writes in cursive better than I do. She started asking us what different things were called, so this went back and forth in both languages. After that, we sat at a table and started coloring. Alla wanted us to write out the English alphabet and Francesca wrote out the Spanish alphabet. Alla was so interested and practiced pronouncing everything we were telling her; she is really bright. She even made us flowers from folded paper. Francesca made Alla a paper crane. Two other girls sat and watched, but did not say much. One had drawn a picture that I found out was of me. It is actually pretty good so I took it home with me.

I think the Orphanage is also a day care because some of the children had their parents pick them up. The workers said some stay at night and others go home and come back in the morning. Makes me wonder!

Today was a great day. I know I am going to love my internship. Despite feeling uncomfortable at first, we are now doing things and it is going to be so great! Tomorrow I am bringing them some markers and coloring books.

Tonight for dinner I ate triple what I normally eat. Olga made stir-fry with green and red peppers, left over cutlets from last night, and some sausage. From there she added pasta and cooked it. Then, she put egg and milk and cream cheese and the stir-fry together, grated cheese over it and cooked it until the eggs were done. It was good. Now that Olga sees how much I can potentially eat, she may want me to eat more and more.

Off to bed early tonight. The alarm clock from home does not work, perhaps the one in my phone will! Oh, Yeah, Mom, that watch you got the battery for, well the strap broke as I was getting off the plane in Helsinki, so no watch for me. I hope to get online and post more pictures tomorrow. Goodnight, with love, Sasha.

## WEDNESDAY- JULY 8:

Studying cases in the Russian language. There are six, with different endings for nouns and adjectives for both male and female, neuter and plural. They are all different for each case as are the pronouns and possessive pronouns. Ugh! It's awful!

Painting class is always fun and a relief after language class. We're working on painting our plates. Our teacher was selling some of her artwork at half price and I bought a small plaque of a Russian scene. Only 300 rubles; 10 dollars. After school and internship, I went to the University to upload pictures.

I made it home safely, same bus as last night, so for the most part I have the route to and from school all set. For the amount of buses and cars, the air quality in the city is pretty nice. At bus stations, you usually find someone with a cigarette, a beer, or both. So many people smoke. It must be a European thing. I hate the smoke! I have been here six days now and my sense of time has changed. It is just two different worlds between here and home. Here time seems so slow and at home I feel like no time is passing at all. Dinner, again, was something new and interesting. It looked like dumplings, but was more of a perogie with what seemed like spicy hamburger in the middle. It was in a chicken broth with crème on top, very good! Hope you enjoy my pictures. Love, Sasha

## THURSDAY- JULY 9:

Now I have taken 727 pictures. I know I have an obsession with photography. I just love capturing things on film. It's my thing! I can't wait to go to St. Petersburg. Today school was awful, test was bad. I get into the test, forget endings, and mix everything up. After the test, the teacher made a nice chart of endings for all six cases. Having the information displayed in this fashion really helped me understand things better. Therefore, for homework tonight, I am going to work on making more charts. Art class was so much fun. After classes, we went on a tour of Yaraslov's Court. We walked across the river. Liza kept yelling at us to stop taking pictures. There were lots of churches and things to see. After our walking tour, the group ended up back at the Pizza place where we had gone a few days ago. I think altogether, I must have walked 5 hours. Masha and I say we are training for our walking tour of St. Petersburg.

Masha and her host go for an "evening stroll" every night and so I accompanied them. We walked along the river in a direction we had not been before. In front of a statue, there were three young people sitting and the one in the middle was playing a guitar. They were all singing. I think they were a band. It sounded nice. It's a great city! So beautiful; especially at night. We passed a hotel and a school and I asked Lena (Masha's host) if we could walk to the monastery at the end of the street. It is a very beautiful place and I enjoyed the feeling there. The trees, the greenery, the smells and the sounds. Awesome!!

Tomorrow we go to Staraya Rusa, two hours away. Located here is the home of Dostayevski (sp), a famous Russian artist and painter. We get a tour of his house and eat dinner. Afterwards I will go to Masha and Lena's house to study for a little while, and go for another walk. Masha will be staying at my house since Olga will be away and said I could have friends spend the night! It will be a fun-filled weekend. Next weekend... St. Petersburg.

While on the tour in the city, we ate at a party house. It was a big place that looked like it hosted many parties. I had borsch for the first time. For those who do not know, it is made with beets. It smelled amazing and the color was so pretty. We were served the borsch first, then some chicken and rice as the second dish, then a small pastry with tea. It was different than I expected it to be. I thought it would be thicker and have more beets in it. A Russian who doesn't like borsch would be a crazy Russian.

Michelle, Steve and I walked around town, went to a Telecom to check our e-mails, then to a *Baskin Robins* for ice cream. We purchased a quart of Rocky Road, sat and ate the whole thing. We were laughing because all the Russians were buying little pints and we Americans had a quart. Art class is over and in its place will be Russian History class; along with the language class. On one of our walks, Adrian, Steve, and I walked to the Barista Hotel, a few steps down and across from school. Liza said there are cute souvenir shops. We go in and this hotel had everything in it. We saw signs that advertised for a dentist, a spa, a nightclub, a pool. It had a bar and restaurant. I ended up buying one of those nesting dolls; the ones you open and there are smaller ones inside. It has a Lion King pattern on it ... I bought it because Lion King is one of my favorite movies. It cost 375 rubles. I almost bought a Harry Potter one: You can find all sorts of people on these dolls, from the Beatles to Obama.

Olga is going to the country for the weekend. She left to-night at 6:30 and will not be back until Sunday night or Monday morning. Apparently, she is with her aunt and mother. When I got home around 6:00, she had dinner ready and then showed me what she had cooked for me for the rest of the weekend, along with directions. Right now, I am home alone as Olga took Shira and Beesha with her. Dinner was cabbage roll stuffed with rice. Last night I had told Olga that I love apple pie, so she went out and bought some apple pie pastry for me. My friends arrive later to spend the night and hang out.

## First Day of History Class:

It has been humid for the past couple days. I feel all gross and sticky. I actually miss air-conditioning. School is going better; I actually understand the uses for the cases in language class. Art is finished and I miss it.

Now we have Russian history class. Our teacher is named Stas (Stanislov) and he runs many of the logistics of the program and deals with our internships, so he is more than just our history teacher.

He begins by telling us about the geography and environment of Russia and how they have influenced its large history. Much of the new information I had never heard before. For instance, Russia does not have any natural borders, and therefore, has always had to have a strong army for defense. The U.S. has ocean on both sides, and two neighbors. Russia has 18 countries that surround its borders and is at risk of invasion because it is a flat, huge land. It does not have mountains, channels, seas, or anything like them to separate it from other countries as in Europe. What it does have is its cold climate. Many enemies have attributed defeat to the cold.

The climate of Russia allows for only 100 days of agriculture and farming. Russia has many natural resources, including 10% oil, 30% gas, and supplies 1/3 of Western Europe's gas. Stas believes that in the next ten to twenty years, the future of world politics will be decided by natural resources. (Oil and gas). He said the American economic crisis is bad for Russia because it is not profitable because we are not buying gas and other natural resources. Stas posed a good question: What is the real value of the economy? Is it lots of money and many zeros after a number on a piece of paper, or is it natural resources or goods, a factory or modern transport? Stas believes that the real value of the economy is natural resources. You may not live as lavishly, or as richly as Americans or other countries that are wealthier than Russia, but at least Russia has natural resources. It was interesting to discuss and think about. It is also interesting to hear a Russian citizen's perspective. Stas has been to America three times. He speaks English very well. He loves to read American mystery novels and watch American TV shows like "House MD."

After history class, we decided to go to the Pizza place. I got an expresso, and then ordered something at random from the menu… it turned out to be a small salad. Steve, Doug and I were there for about 45 minutes then left to walk to the University, about 15 minutes away. It took longer this time because a drunken Russian man looking for money accompanied us. He had cigarettes in one hand and you could smell the alcohol on his breath. He was asking us where we were from. Steve tried to tell him that we did not understand Russian. He kept following us. I decided to be on the other side of the sidewalk and up a little ways from the guys just to keep my distance from him. It was awkward and uncomfortable. I was worried that as he was talking to us, someone else might be trying to go through our bags. Steve was trying to get rid of the person and suggested we go to the Adidas store. When we go in, I tell Doug, I bet the guy just waits for us, and that's exactly what he did. Oh, Man!!! Eventually, when he asked us where we were going, Doug pointed in the opposite direction and the person went that way! When we came out of the store, Steve said the guy had American money in his hand, and made motions with his fingers like shooting up his arm with a needle. We do not know if he was trying to get money or drugs from us, or if he wanted us to buy from him. Thankfully, he was just annoying and did not do us any harm. Being harassed by a Russian drunk is certainly interesting. So that's been my day. I had dinner with Olga. It's nice to have her back. She spent the weekend at her Dacha, which is 150km away, about 2 hours. She came home with buckets and bags full of produce and fruit. For dinner, we had stuffed cabbage.

There are 24-hour flower shops everywhere. At the bus stops, there are mini markets where you can buy alcohol, nail polish, hair products, playing cards, small toys, magazines, small purses, wallets, even snacks. Some of them have ATM's also. I would never purchase anything from them, but it is still interesting. Personally, I don't know what occasion would warrant having to buy flowers in the middle of the night, so the idea of a 24-hour flower shop seems somewhat silly.

History class was tiring today. For some reason I have always had trouble staying awake in lectures; unless it was Anatomy, Russian, or a Science/Nursing class. Today, we were talking about the formation of the Russian state as told in the Russian Chronicles. This included information about the first Russian princes: Riurik, Oleg, Igor, Olga, Swiatoslav, Vladimir, and Karoslav. Olga was the first Christian ruler of Russia, after her husband, Igor, was murdered. Other interesting facts: the name Russia comes from "Rus" (or maybe "Russ"), either way pronounced as "ros," as in "roster." Russia was baptized by Vladimir and adopted Christianity. The first written law was established by Jaroslav (pronounced "Yaroslav," I believe). I usually do not prefer history, but this is very interesting and I actually enjoy learning about it.

After history class, we went to a studio to weave baskets. Our teacher's name was Vladimir and he is Matt's host father. He has been weaving for 26 years. He had previously spent a year traveling all over America, teaching students in our country how to make baskets. He has written a book about it that can be purchased on Amazon and he said, next spring he is going back to America to teach weaving again.

Our birch bark baskets took about 2-3 hours to make a small one. At first, I did not think it would take that long, but it is very tedious. Once you get the bottom, corners, and sides set up, it is easier from then on. I do remember that we had to put vegetable oil on the birch bark so it would bend and be easier to use. We used 12 pieces to make a 6 by 6 basket. Overall, it was fun and relaxing. The place where the studio was located had a church and other buildings around it and was pretty. It was in a part of the city I had never walked in before. Novgorod is truly beautiful!

When I got home, Olga and I had dinner. She left to get a manicure, which I thought was interesting. Clothes here are ridiculous in price! I wonder what Russians think about our "cheap" prices. Tomorrow we go on another trip to some type of museum.

For breakfast, I had pasta with eggs... very good. School was good and during history class, we all went to the local Art Museum near the Kremlin. It had many works by local artists as well as other things pertaining to the history of Novgorod and Russia. There was so much!

Afterwards, Masha, Doug, Steve, Adrian and I decided to go to a coffee shop called Coffee Land, and their slogan was "Tea and Life." The style of the shop was European, and Michael Jackson was playing on the radio. I guess Russia is still mourning. Looking through the menu, we came across a breakfast item called, "Big English Breakfast." It consisted of omelet with roast bacon, sausages, field mushrooms, and toast. It was amusing what was considered an English breakfast.

First, we started with coffee drinks. I had an orange dream (orange juice with expresso, caramel syrup, and ice). There was a green cherry in it. Bad taste. After coffee, we were still hungry and asked for the menu again while we were laughing. They must have thought, "Silly Americans." Another thing on the menu was "Thawy in the Mouth" ... yes, "thawy." It was ice cream wrapped in a hot pancake. This thawy dessert arrives, big and delicious looking, topped with whipped cream, shaves of chocolate, a mint leaf, and orange glaze with white raisins. The ways to prepare blini are endless. Masha and I shared it and I ended up eating the mint leaf. From Coffee Land we went to the bank and then to the university to post pictures, then on to home.

As I went up the stairs at home, I could hear a lot of noise coming from Olga's house and there was a smell of smoke. The house was filled with smoke and I wondered what had burned. The living room and my room were closed, but I could see Olga cooking in the kitchen. Meanwhile, the house filled with guests: Olga's childhood friend, Ilena, and her daughter, Masha, visiting from a town north near St. Petersburg. The friend's mother is a neighbor, Later, another friend arrived, Tatianna. For dinner, Olga went all out, setting up a big table in the living room. Olga prepared a soup that had five different types of meat as well as a few vegetables. It was delicious. She made these pita-looking things filled with meat, cheese, and dill. This is what caused the smoke. Olga's food never ceases to please me. I ate too much. For dessert, we had tea and vanilla ice cream.

The tea was too hot to drink. There is a Russian tradition: when the tea is too hot, you pour some onto the saucer and drink from there. I felt funny slurping tea from a saucer.

After tea and ice cream, Masha and I went into my bedroom to talk... she knew a little English. The first thing she asked me was, "How do you feel about the death of Michael Jackson?" I was amused that this was the first thing she asked me! I told her I thought it was sad; that he was a great performer. Masha responded by saying she thought he was killed. Masha went on to tell me about herself. She is 17 and has played the violin for 6 years and is currently in a band. She shared some of her band's music and pictures with me. We went through some of the music on my computer. She was interested in what I listen to. From there she wanted to have tea again, so we went back into the living room. I worked on my homework, while she helped me with pronunciations. She said the key to learning is to repeat words over and over.

When I was not talking with Masha, I spent time listening to the women all get together and speak. I recognized many words, but it was hard putting them together to figure out what was going on. I understand they only get together once or twice a year. Overall, it was a nice evening and it was nice to have someone to speak English and Russian with who was around my age.

I have come to realize eating here is an event. Russians spend much time preparing food, down to the monotonous chopping of vegetables and meats. They are very offended if you do not eat what you are offered. Since they left I am packing for St. Petersburg. That is all for now. Sasha

## PETERHOF AND PUSHKIN: SUMMER AND WINTER PALACES OF PETER THE GREAT

The first place on our journey today was Peterhof, located in the suburbs of St. Petersburg. Peterhof is one of my favorite places. I love nature, gardens, and flowers, so I was happy here. Peter the Great had wanted to have more gardens and fountains than the Palace at Versailles. There were hundreds. Some fountains were "trick" fountains. Some places had stone pathways and if you stepped on the wrong stone, you got wet. We were supposed to watch our guide; she knew where they were. That was easier said than done. I got wetter than anyone else did.

From here, we piled into our van, which, by the way, was a purple Mercedes. Amazing!! We headed to Pushkin, where we toured the castle, which was huge and very pretty. Pushkin is also known as "Tsarskoe Selo." The name Pushkin is after one of the most famous Russian writers, Alexander Pushkin. The palace is similar to the summer palace... lots of gold. Most of the world's Amber (made from hardened tree sap) is located around the Baltic Sea. This palace is famous for its Amber Room. When we were touring the insides of these palaces, we had to put booties on our shoes, like surgeons wear. This helps keep the marble and wood floors in good condition, but it was slippery. I noticed that in these palaces, the architecture is different in every room and there are paintings and intricate carvings all over. The detail and effort put into these buildings is phenomenal and so impressive.

## St. Petersburg:

Driving into the city, the road turned into a multilane highway with ramps, much like American cities. I saw a Ford dealership and about three McDonald's before we got to our stop. Our bus stopped in front of the metro, near a huge building with fountains and a statue of Lenin. I found out later, that the metro in St. Petersburg is the deepest in the world, at 90 meters. It runs below the canals and waterways of the city. Riding the metro was a bit of a whirlwind, having never been on one before, and trying to keep up with Liza. I locked up my book bag and had all my documents under my sweatshirt. My money was clipped to my belt and tucked inside my pants. We were warned about gypsies coming out of nowhere and trying to pickpocket you. However, we did not see any gypsies. Later, someone said they were a bigger problem five years ago. Our hostel/hotel was located at 16 Nevsky Prospekt (avenue). After a long metro ride, we walked 10 minutes to our hotel, which was three minutes from the winter palace.

We checked in, dropped off our stuff and ate at this fast food place across the street. I ate blini with salmon and then kasha, which is like porridge. I liked both. While in this place, we ended up sitting next to a woman and her son who spoke English. Come to find out they had been traveling around Europe and were spending 6 days in St. Petersburg. They were from Greenbay, Wisconsin; the son goes to Mercyhurst College. After chatting with them, we headed out for our walking tour, which took about 5 hours. It is a city split into five islands by the Neva, Big Neva, Big Nevka, and Small Nevka Rivers. It is a major trade center and shipping center, and has many shipyards. There are over 500 bridges. The main bridges go up at 2am, so we must remember this or we could spend the night on one of the islands.

On our tour, we saw many newlyweds getting their pictures taken by a statue, well, or building. One couple had their first dance by the river. At first, I thought it would be neat to be married in this city... not so neat... too many people, only a few feet from each other. It's quite comical! One bride seemed somewhat jealous of the other couple when her husband did not carry her over the bridge they were near.

A restaurant we ate in was a Russian place pronounced "Yolki Palki." I felt like I was in a forest in a fairy tale. It had a tree and folk decorations. The food was good (fish soup). When the whole group of us came in, two Russian couples got up and left. I wonder if we were intimidating to them?

Masha and I had our room on the fourth floor and everyone else was in an apartment above us that had a kitchen, living/dining area and four rooms with beds. Masha and I hung out with the others until 3am. The sun was coming up when we went to bed.

Four days in St. Petersburg! The city only gets 60 days of bright clear sunny days a year. It is located next to the Gulf of Finland. I think this is so neat... far north; almost to the Artic circle There are many beautiful churches; some with gorgeous looking domes, mostly in gold, gray, or blue. More fountains and pretty gardens. I noticed a group of tourists huddled together looking at something. I was curious, and realized it was a little squirrel begging for food. I squatted down and got him to come up to my hand twice. I affectionately named him, Boris. He was adorable. He made my day!

When we got to our rooms (home away from home), we rested, got dressed up, and ate. It is funny, we come to this great Russian city and most of the time was spent eating non-Russian food. At Pizza Hut, we ordered a Hawaiian pizza. The restaurant was playing American music and had American decorations.

From here it is on to the ballet; a 20 minute walk in dress shoes. How do Russian women deal with high heels every day? The ballet was "Swan Lake" by Tchaikovsky. This performance was one of the most impressive aspects of visiting this city. I guess it must be my love of anatomy coming back to me as I watch the ballerina's amazingly strong muscles. We had box seats; the orchestra was great. I love listening to live

music. Doug, who is a dancer, says that the lead female ballerina is well on her way to needing some type of joint replacement soon and went on to describe how ballet ruins the
body and wears it out from the demanding routines. Their
joints have to go out of the normal range of motion. Again, I
think back to anatomy class and feel a bit uncomfortable
thinking of what they go through in order to perform so beau-
tifully.

Afterwards, we go back home and change our outfits, then
go to Subway, another American place! From here, Masha and
I took a boat ride on the canals and river. It cost 500 rubles a
person, a bit pricey, but worth it. We were on the boat until
2:30 am. It was very enjoyable and fun. A mix of Russian
techno music and American music by Whitney Houston,
Justin Timberlake and others was playing.

The city is beautiful; very European in style and flavor. It
is different from Novgorod. It is very large and we walk a lot.
In four days I did the following: Three hour walking tour of
the city, a tour of St. Issac's, a tour of the Hermitage, a tour of
Peterhof and Pushkin, Russian ballet, boat ride on the canals,
tour of the Cathedral of the Spilled Blood, and lots of sightseeing and eating. I cannot begin to describe how beautiful
this city is. I think cities are more beautiful at night when they
are all lit up. One night on a walk, we saw fireworks. There is
always someone performing something in the square in front
of the palace.

## ST. ISSAC'S CATHEDRAL AND THE HERMITAGE

St. Issac was the patron saint of Peter the Great. The cathedral was beautiful... lots of gold, mosaics, icons, chandeliers and huge bronze doors with sculptures. The doors are so
large they have only been opened once or twice. On our trav-
els, we saw more newlyweds. The Hermitage is basically an
art museum... breathtaking! There is so much art and things

to look at that if you spent one minute looking at each, it would take three years. Yes, three years, 24 hours a day! So much stuff. So phenomenal! Most awesome was being able to see art by famous artists; being so close you could touch it.

In the Hermitage, I saw original works by Picasso, Monet, DaVinci, Michaelangelo, Rembrandt, Cezanne, Goya, and a lot more. Mom, I thought of you as I looked at all the artwork and took pictures. I also bought myself my very own Russian white leather and fox fur winter hat.

After seeing the Hermitage, Liza recommended we eat at a pie place, as she called it. It is a German restaurant and they make "pies." I would not call them "pies." However, these "pies" can be filled with all sorts of things from meat to mushrooms to fruit. I tried one filled with rabbit and mushrooms. The rabbit reminded me of chicken. The mushrooms were amazing; the best I have had in my life.

Last day in St. Petersburg. Masha and I slept in. We decided to spend the last day going to the Church of the Savior of Blood. It was built over the spot where Alexander II was shot and murdered. Inside, the walls were all mosaics. Gorgeous! Masha and I did a little souvenir shopping, then walked in a park next to the church.

In Russia, there are pigeons everywhere. In various places in St. Petersburg, there are people with animals such as monkeys, hawks, baby foxes, and a lynx cub in captivity so people can take pictures of them. I am sure it is illegal in the U.S., as it should be. I feel bad for the animals and wonder what happens to them when they are not wanted any more. They cannot be released into the wild because they would surely die.

I will miss the city, but four days was enough. The ride home was spent sleeping and looking out the window at the countryside while listening to music. The houses or dachas along the countryside are cute and come in an array of colors.

They have intricate woodwork around the windows, doors, and eaves. I thought, "This country is so big and the city is only a few hours away from Novgorod, yet it feels so different from Novgorod." It is humbling in that I really get a sense of how small I am compared to the huge world around me. It is harder to notice it at home in the U.S., but here I think about it a lot. Being in a foreign country, seeing the differences among people, goes to show how small one person is in the whole world... a good reminder that I am connected to something much bigger than I can imagine. When I arrived home, Olga had food waiting for me... noodles and chicken leg. We sat on the couch, talked about my trip. Showed her some pictures, and went to bed. I love so much about this country.

## BACK TO THE DAILY ROUTINE JULY 20TH

Back to school again. History class was interesting. We talked about paganism and different Russian pagan traditions. Stas began by saying paganism was in the historical past of every nation.

We learned that Swarog was the god creator, Stribog the god of the upper world and winds, Dazhdbog, the god of justice and the giver of sun and day. Perun was the god of storms, thunder, and lightning. Domovoi was the spirit of the home who was invisible and lived under the stove or in the attic. He was the protector of the house; brought tranquility, linked horses, cattle, milk, and, bread, and if you made him angry in any way, he would leave your home. This was considered very bad! Leshi was the god of the forest and Vodoanoi was the water spirit. Other Russian superstitions include the following:

The cat is the most spiritual creature so he must be the first to enter a new home. If you do not have a cat, you must borrow your neighbor's and push him over the threshold.

If you meet a woman with two empty baskets in her hand, this is bad luck. If they are full, this is a good omen. If you come across a burial procession this is good for you... in that you are still living. If you leave a key on the table or any place it is not supposed to be, it is bad luck because the key had a special place, a nail on the wall.

If you drop a knife you will have a quarrel, drop a fork and you have a male visitor, drop a spoon and you will have a female visitor. If your left hand itches, you'll receive money. If the tip of your nose itches, you are supposed to drink vodka.

When traveling if you forget something and return to retrieve it... bad luck. Whistling in the house is prohibited because you will lose money.

A sauna is considered a dirty place and women are supposed to give birth here and not in the home because the home is sacred and must not be placed in danger by unclean, evil spirits. A woman, who is giving birth, soon after, is an open door for good and evil spirits. Overall an interesting lecture.

After school, I went to Francesca's house, had some tea and vegetables, and took a small nap before our internship. When we got to the orphanage, it was raining hard, so we went under some outdoor hut-like structures that had tables and benches. All the children seemed interested in talking to us. Even the boys came up to us. They definitely are not as reserved as they used to be.

At home, Olga said Liza was coming over. Liza, my Russian teacher, and Olga had been friends for a long time. For dinner, we had salad with ham, other vegetables, with dill, all chopped and diced. With it, we had bread water, Kvas. It looked like root beer, but did not taste like it. It is carbonated. I did not like it at all.

Before Liza arrived, I watched Olga cook. She made apple "perok" or pie. Instead of the traditional piecrust, she used tortillas. Inside she put the cut slices of apple, cinnamon, sugar, and egg sauce, and something that looked like cream cheese. She then baked it all. When you ate it, you could not tell it was tortilla shells. Amazing. It was moist and flavorful. We had a new flavor of tea: chamomile and apple.

## Wooden Architecture Museum:

During history class, we went to the Museum of Popular Wooden Architecture, outside Novgorod. It was filled with various buildings made of all wood... no nails at all. I was thinking these were the original log homes. Apparently, this style was used by pagans and folk people. The museum was in the center of countryside, surrounded by woods and open grass, with water on three sides, by a lake and a river. There were even churches, a well, and some boats all made of wood, without any nails. Nice trip. Mosquitoes were bad.

When we got back, we went to Coffee Land and I did my homework until it was time for my internship. Francesca and I colored with the kids and tried to talk more with them.

Olga apparently works at some place with computers and deals with legal clients. She enters data. I also found out that Olga is also a nurse, plays piano, and another traditional Russian instrument, has been a teacher and a manager. I wonder, is there anything Olga cannot do? She is amazing! Reminds me of you, Mom.

We went to Scoff, a 6-hour ride there and back. At Scoff, there is a monastery and catacombs. Monks are buried in the catacombs and their bodies somehow were preserved.

Internship was great fun today. The children were watching "Snow White" in Russian when we arrived. We colored and played volleyball. The workers were also interested in speaking with me today. They told me that the American banks had failed, and I asked, "Now?" They laughed and said, "No, in the fall and winter." Then they asked if my parents worked. I told them my parents did not work (I did not know the word for 'retired'), so they thought I was rich. I had to tell them my parents' ages and then they understood. Our next trip was to see the oldest stone fortress in Russia.

## PSKOV: A MONASTERY, FORTRESS AND A KREMLIN:

At the monastery are limestone caves where monks are buried. When you go in, you are given a candle and are accompanied by a monk. If you are claustrophobic, this is not the place for you. It would be a good setting for a horror movie. After the caves, we went into a small church. Three monks came in and got ready to say their prayers. We had other places to go so we did not hear them do their chants.

The monastery felt like such a peaceful place, I could have spent much more time there. I have always thought that monks and deeply religious people who devote their lives to God are extremely fascinating. I wish I had a deeper faith, with their dedication and focus. Being in their presence and visiting the monastery was an awesome experience.

The Kremlin here is much smaller than the one in Novgorod. When we arrived, it was time for church to begin. The bells from the bell tower began to chime and we soon realized something special was going on. There were many Orthodox priests in attendance, the church was decorated elaborately, and a red carpet was rolled out. It was neat to be here to see this display for the Archbishop.

The book I am reading is called, "My Stroke of Insight." It is about a doctor who has a stroke and writes about how she was able to recover from the stroke and how her life changed.

It is written so anyone can understand the terminology and medical aspects. You should Google it and look into it.

Of course, when I got home I had a nice meal waiting for me: a vegetable stir-fry with potatoes and chicken, along with a new apple pastry.

## ICONS:

Luckily, in history class we went back to the Archeological museum in the Kremlin and looked at many icons. The oldest date back to the 13th century. Many are of St. Nickolas and St, George, popular saints in the Orthodox Church. Many depicted scenes from the life of Jesus. Some showed "The Old Testament Trinity." I do not know if this refers to the same trinity as I know it. The Orthodox Church places emphasis on the life of Jesus and the many miracles he performed. It does not emphasize the crucifixion as much as the Catholic Church does.

After class, we went in search of free internet service and came to an Italian restaurant, Napoli. Steve and I ordered minestrone soup. A bottle of water cost 3 dollars. Overall, it was a nice place to sit and use the internet. Steve and I joked that we looked like typical Americans with our big laptops, sitting in a restaurant for three hours borrowing the internet.

When I got home and ate dinner, Masha came over and we headed for an Irish Pub near the Kremlin, called Greensleeves. The others joined us. We watched the flat screen plasma TV that was playing Eric Clapton in concert. After the pub, Masha, Steve, Magna, Jim, and Matt came over. We got out of the pub at 11:30, walked to the nearest bus stop, and waited almost an hour and the bus never showed up. We called a taxi. The taxi driver was playing old Britney Spears on the radio. We hung out in the kitchen at my house talking, eating and discussing religion.

## AMERICAN STYLE BARBECUE JULY 26TH:

Today everyone is invited to a barbecue at a man named Sean's house. Don knows Sean, an older man who has lived in Novgorod about 10 years. He is originally from the U.S. Sean works with American and Russian universities and hosts people at his house. He also has a website: US-Russian nurses.com. He lives on the outskirts where there are many small cottages. His house is a pretty blue. Inside it had wooden floors, walls, and ceilings. The bathroom was larger than most bathrooms; one wall all mirrors, with blue tile on the floor. Items in the house looked quite expensive. He showed Masha and me a Matroshka doll that he had custom made in Moscow (the birthplace ofMatroshka dolls). He designed it and an artist made it for him. There was a doll for each of his parents and his brother. Really neat!!

Outside was a small deck and small yard. There were about 20 people there. Sean had devised a tournament with eight teams of two. We drew numbers to find our partner. We played darts, horseshoes, boggle, uno, and badminton. There were many snacks and for dinner, we had kabobs made with meat, onions, bread, tomatoes, cucumbers, and dill. Kabobs in Russian are pronounced "Shoshleek."

During the party, I talked with Yuri quite a bit. He is 23 and speaks English, Russian, and some Spanish. He is going to school to be a doctor and will finish in two years. We discussed health care. Apparently, doctors in Russia are paid less than nurses and that non-college people and those who work their way up in a random job, make more money than doctors. Yuri is not sure if he wants to incorporate his language skills with his work, yet, because he would earn more money that way.

I began thinking about perhaps combining my nursing job with Russian language; if I ever become fluent in it. It would take a long time, but we will see. Sean mentioned that he works with U.S. nurses that know Russian and hosts conferences for them. I felt that this is so ironic... that this is what Sean does. I go to Russia; meet someone who works with nursing and the Russian language. Got me to thinking about all the options there are for nurses.

After the party at Sean's, Don's host, Sasha and his wife invited us to their home to hang out some more. They had a small pavilion in their back yard and a small grill. Sasha grilled some hot dogs. The guys brought some beer and we sat around talking. Yuri and Steve sang some songs. It was funny because Steve was singing in half Russian and half Spanish. It was a great night. We called a taxi to get home.

## E-MAIL FROM ALEX TO HOME... JULY 27TH:

Hello Mom, Nice to hear from you! The swelling in my legs is better and I have been drinking more water. I agree with you that I am dehydrated. Russians do not drink much water. They do not have bottles with them all the time as I do at home.

Over the weekend, I went to a party at this 50-60 year old person's house, Sean McGivern. I feel like maybe in the future I may combine Russian and nursing. That would give me more chances to come back to Russia in the future and then go to Moscow to research my heritage. It is impossible to do that on this trip. Everything is planned and scheduled. It is crazy how things happen. I am thinking it is all part of God's plan how I met all these people in my field.

As for your upcoming surgery, it sounds like a good thing. I hope that eventually, you can get the trachea out!

One last thing: Liza was visiting Olga the other day and Olga told her how amazed and proud she is of how far I am in my life. She said that if I had stayed here, I might never have gone to school. Olga is amazed that I am going to be a nurse and that I am back visiting Russia. Olga also said she could tell that you were such a stable and driving force in my life. (I talk to her a lot about you.) Wow, that was really nice that Olga said that!

From what Olga said it made me miss you a lot and I want to say that I do agree with what she says: you have been the stability in my life and that without it I would not be where I am. I cannot thank you enough. I know that many times, I am selfish and unappreciative, but I hope you know how much it means. I feel so blessed to have you.

## E-MAIL FROM ALEX TO HOME... JULY 28TH:

Hello Mom, Yeah, that Sean guy was very interesting. I also met a young man named Yuri. He is 23 and going to be a doctor in 2 years. I spent a lot of time talking to him about medicine here and in the states. I will write more in my blog.

Last night I told Olga that you mentioned her in an e-mail and said, "Hello." She brightened up so much and kept saying a big "thank you" over and over. She told me she thanks you from the bottom of her heart for bringing me to the United States from Moscow. I can tell that she was very sincere. It was the sweetest thing. She is an amazing woman. I should tell you she is also a nurse. She has done so many things in her life... reminds me of you. She is very determined and independent. Tonight we are having borsch; tomorrow, liver. Talk to you soon. Love, Alex

## HISTORY CLASS:

The Mongols attacked in 1223 and 1239, but Novgorod was never taken. In the 12th century, Novgorod achieved independence. It was private land and the prince had no right to buy land in the territory. The foundations of Moscow:

Moscow was relatively secure from attack compared to the rest of Russia. It had a favorable geographic location for travel, but had poor soil. The term Czar came from the Russian form of Caesar. The last part of class we talked about current relations between Russia and America. Stas says there is an anti-American feeling ever since Serbia, Kosovo, and Yugoslavia. He thinks actions against Yugoslavia were a huge mistake. It is his opinion that America missed a chance to better relations directly after 9/11. (Putin was the first foreign leader to call President Bush after the attacks). Russians feel sorry for Americans, but not for America.

Stas went on to say that, Russia is wary of the gap between the real intention of the American government and the ideal of democracy and often wonders how big it is. Lastly, Stas voiced his own opinions of Obama. He began by saying that Obama's success is everything opposite of Bush. Personally, he would have voted for McCain only because McCain openly and directly claims his intentions. Stas said he was shocked when Obama won. Despite the anti view of Americans, I have never felt any hostility towards myself while in this country. Always a positive experience.

After class, we went to a local convent in Novgorod. The convent is noted for miracles. The church is the burial place of Saint Varlam. During ancient times, Ivan the Terrible came here to pray. He wanted to open the tomb of the famous saint, the founder of the convent. When he went to do this, the tomb caught on fire and he knew that it was not the right thing to do... Currently, all the nuns who live here grow all their own food. They sell a small amount for a little money. We toured the church and grounds and went up a hill; on top was a small chapel. Many people go there to pray. It is said that if you take intentions for anyone who needs healing, including yourself, say a prayer, and walk around the hill three times, you may receive a miracle. On the grounds there is a well which they say has the cleanest water and is considered holy and to have brought about miracles. We had a drink and washed our faces. It tasted fresh and crisp.

I finally saw a cemetery. It reminded me of the cemeteries in Germany, I had seen in the hometown where my father grew up.

## RUSSIAN CUISINE:

Today we took a boat ride on the Volkhov River and discussed Russian Cuisine.

Factors that influence any cuisine are climate and geography. Most fruits and berries in Russia are limited due to the short growing season. Original menu of a peasant included apples, pears and prunes. There are cranberries and gooseberries that are used for jelly, jams, and a sweetener. There were not a lot of meat products, as cattle were important.

Peasants were known for eating many milk products, which is an influence from Turkey. Sour cream is put on just about everything.

Peasants did not have a grill or frying pan; only big ovens, so many things were stewed. This is why so much of Russian cuisine consists of soups and porridges.

Bread is made from rye and is brown. Kvas is a drink made from fermented bread. Boiled grains are known as porridge or kasha. Rice is used for special meals. It plays an important role in the ritual meal at a wake. It is similar to rice pudding. There is a saying, "You can't make porridge with him," meaning that this person is not your friend.

Vodka was everyone's favorite part of the lecture. It means, "Little water" and is made from fermented grain and distilled, then filtered two or three times. Monks created the first vodka for medicinal use in the 15th century. They had the time, the education, and extra bread. Originally, it was an herbal type medicine. The State claimed a monopoly on the production and selling of Vodka and it became 1/3rd of the income of the State from the 15-20th century. There is a joke about increasing vodka prices:

Son: "Dad, if prices of vodka go up does that mean we'll drink less?"

Father: "No, son, we eat less."

In World War II, soldiers received 100g of vodka a day in their rations. If a soldier died, his ration would go to the remaining soldiers.

Mushroom picking is known as "White Hunting" and is a common pastime. They are used in soup, sauces, and can be fried, dried, salted and marinated.

Vegetables are commonly salted or marinated with salt, water, herbs, black currant leaves and horseradish. Cabbage is used as a base for soups. The simplest soup consists of onion, cabbage, and water. Potatoes only became a part of the meal in the 18th century. People were ordered by the military to grow potatoes. The potato took the place of the turnip.

After the 18th century, meat was eaten in smaller pieces. Normally it would be cooked in the ovens and eaten as a whole piece.

Caviar is a traditional Russian meal. Black caviar is from sturgeon; red caviar is from salmon. Some fry it.

Pelmeni is eaten a lot. It is meat with pasta and originally a Finnish meal. It looks like tortellini with meat inside. Sausage was a way to preserve meat.

Tea, salad, chocolate, and ice cream are not traditionally part of the meal. Tea arrived from china in the 17th century via the Mongols. Tea can be a meal (brunch), with jam, honey, dry fruit, bread, and blini. Sugar and tea are eaten separately; you do not put the sugar in the tea, but eat it alongside the tea. Thus, sugar cubes.

During the 18th century chopped meat, macaroni, and sauces were introduced. German, British, and French imported cookware allowed for different ways of food preparation.

Salad, to my surprise was not traditional. Except for soup, nothing was ever mixed together in a bowl. Salad originated in the houses of French Aristocrats and spread, so that by the 20th century everyone was eating salad.

## HISTORY CLASS:

Today was World War II from a Russian perspective. Stas started by pointing out some important dates:

- June 22nd 1941-- Russia enters the war

- December 7th 1941-- United States enters war

- May 8th 1945-- Victory Day, U.S. and Europe

- May 9th 1945-- Victory Day Russia (Last battle for Prague)

- September 2nd 1945-- End of Russian campaign

The material effect of the war was very extensive and grave. Novgorod was demolished and is currently much smaller than before the war. Statistics on how much the Germans destroyed in Russia: 32,000 factories, 4,000 railroad stations, 38,000 hospitals, 82,000 schools, 400 museums, and 43,000 libraries. Russia lost 1/3rd of its national treasures; the Soviet Union was disintegrated; the Ukraine and others became free. The most valuable loss was lives. The officially recognized number is 27 million. Of that, 11 million was military. To put that in perspective, the U.S. lost 250,000 in the war. Of the 27 million that died, most were of reproductive age; 18 to

20 years later, there is still a big population gap. The war was more of a psychological shock. It was a patriotic war; the question of life over death. The Russians understood that the intention of the Germans was to kill everyone.

Stas gave us some personal stories of the War. Stas's father is Ukrainian and his mother Bela-Russian, from Belarus. His father was also half Jew. During the war, Stas's father was seven years old. Stas's grandfather was an officer in the Red Army and worked as a medic. Stas's father survived only by chance. The family that offered their home to Stas's father, taught the children to jump into a hole under the house whenever they saw German soldiers. They were told not to go outside the confines of the yard. It was to their advantage that the Germans never spent more than 2 or 3 nights in a village. In the village, the only cruel thing the Germans did was to kill a boy who had found the binoculars of a German officer. When the officer returned to get them and asked who had taken them, he then shot the boy on the spot.

Three hundred Jews were rounded up and killed 6km from the village. Stas's grandfather, his father's father, was a military doctor from 1932 to the end of the war. On paper, he was with the motorized division, but was actually in the infantry. His grandfather was on leave when all the troops in his division disappeared. His daughter was to have surgery in St. Petersburg. He had received a telegram to come home immediately. When he returned he did not find anyone. He did come across other soldiers from other divisions. He became a commander of M.A.S.H.

Stas's grandfather came back from the war without injury. From records Stas received from him, he learned that 60,000 people came through the hospital his grandfather administered. 2.5% died, the rest were divided, based upon their injuries, and were sent on for further treatment. His grandfather never talked about the war. Stas wonders why he, Stas, a historian, never asked him questions.

The younger brother of Stas's grandfather was a chemical engineer, who volunteered to serve. He was a lieutenant. He eventually disappeared. He has a daughter who was born in 1941 who now lives in Boston; she never knew her father. We were told to keep in mind that 80% of the Germans were destroyed by Russia; only 20% by the U.S. and Britain. It is a story of loss, suffering, and a glorious victory over the Germans. The war is still a money and business maker. Stas's father still receives a small pension from Germany for any emotional damages the war had on him as a boy. When Germany took control of Poland, Lithuania, Estonia, and Latvia, Russia stood by and did nothing. A former Non-Aggression Pact was broken when Germany marched into Russia. Russian schools do not teach children about American and British involvement, Normandy, or the western front. They are not taught anything about events that happened before Russia got involved.

The Holocaust was horrific, but to put things in perspective, not as big as compared to the Russian loss. There should be a balanced focus on the events of the war. I do not remember ever learning about Russia's involvement.

To top off this very good lecture, Stas brought in his grandfather's medals from serving in the war.

Back at home in the evening, I asked Olga a question about the Soviet Union and this led me to looking at a collection of books Olga has. One book about the Soviet Union had pictures, dates, and writings; and a publication date of 1975. I wondered how much was propaganda. Other books in the set included a book about Biology and one about General Anatomy. I had a ball with the anatomy book and took lots of pictures of the figures because I can recognize them from my own anatomy books. Maybe I can learn some Russian names of anatomy. How cool!!

Next day we met Doug at Coffee Land for breakfast at 11:00. We talked about yesterday's history class; I had some questions. I got a good run through of Russian history beginning in 1900, thanks to Doug and Masha. It helps when most of the group are international relations majors or history majors. Stas said he believes in people and diplomacy… that exchange programs, such as I am in, are as useful as a strong missile. If just one person can learn about a country and pass it on to others, it could change false opinions and impressions.

More walking and sightseeing. Language class has ended. We are trying to get some pictures of the city itself. Our walking led us back to the Pizza place where the group met on some of our first days here. Our conversation centered on marriage and relationships. Apparently, in Russia there isn't an engagement period. Traditionally, two people date and then get married. They set a date to sign papers and can do the church thing if they want. In the morning, the couple signs papers; in the afternoon they drive around town and stop at various places to take pictures. Engagement is becoming a bit more popular because of American movies. I noticed a bunch of rice on the ground in front of a restaurant. Lena said you throw money at the feet of a couple to wish them a prosperous marriage and rice for a long, happy marriage.

The group went to get beer, so Don and I waited on a park bench. We talked about how many little children there are in Novgorod. Everywhere you turn, you see someone pushing a stroller or dragging a toddler behind him or her. There are little kids running around everywhere. The children in Russia are all so adorable and cute! Lucky for me; hopefully, I will have some cute kids. Sasha says the government is paying couples so much per child. Apparently, the population rate is so low because families are having only one or two children. Abortion is often used instead of birth control. Some women have had as many as five abortions. Now the government realizes what a negative effect a low birth rate has on the country and is paying to increase its population. Interesting!

## HISTORY CLASS:

Stas's last lecture talked about the divided nature of the Russian people, the Kosaks, and a little about the USSR. For centuries, the Russian people have been oppressed by the State. The law came from the Vikings; then the Mongols. The People of Russian never respected the law and were never a part of its creation. Avoiding the law was the best thing to do. The ruling class then resorted to cruelty. During Perestroika, the State was finally given to the people, but they have a distrust of the State.

Millions of current Russians are descended from the Kosaks, including Andrew, the antique dealer. Kosak refers to frontiersmen who prefer to live alone, freely, in the forest zone... no wives, jobs, family to tie them down. To get by they would hunt, fish, and steal. They did produce salt and sell it for a small amount of money. They were Christian and Slavonic so they robbed mostly the Muslims. They created their own republic; their leaders were Ottomans. To become a Kosak, a man had to proclaim that he was a follower of Christ and make the sign of the cross. Kosaks became connected to the government in the 18th century. They are viewed as strong, powerful, brave men, who were expert horsemen.

The last part of class was open to questions. Masha asked if the Dachas are private or public land. The dachas are private land with a tax of less than 500 rubles a year... about 20 dollars. Half of the people use the dacha as a hobby for growing things; others use it for making a profit by selling produce to make a living. Stas ended by saying that Russians can survive without the State. For centuries, they have survived despite being controlled and avoiding government. Their perseverance and will to live is apparent. The people stick together and know how to survive.

My thoughts: America is great with lots of nice things, but it is a land of convenience, fast food, and getting what you want quickly. There are not many people in my generation who know how to survive like our grandparents did. It seems that even people my age in Russia still learn and use things from their grandparents and parents, but are also willing to learn new ways. Not many young Americans know how to make or preserve things. We would not be prepared for a crisis, as the Russians would be.

We are too concerned about our ipods, computers, and internet. In this age of technology, I personally fear we are becoming too attached and dependent. For extended periods on this trip, I have been free of electronics and it was nice. Mom, you might be shocked to have me say that, because most of the time at home, I am attached to my computer and my telephone. I wish I knew how to cook as well as Olga, how to can fruit and vegetables, use herbs. I have always been too busy to learn from you, Mom, when you offered to teach me.

Anyway, this lecture got me to thinking. History class has been very good. Stas is a very knowledgeable man who loves to tell about his country. I appreciate the balanced way he passes on his wealth of knowledge.

After class, we went to a souvenir shop. From there we had to make one last trip to Coffee Land. Most of the group is leaving and how fast the time has gone by. Liza gave a toast; we drank our mead, and enjoyed our last time together with our teachers. I hate goodbyes and leaving people. I hate when things happen for the last time. I get too sad and nostalgic for my own good.

## THE LAST TWO WEEKS:

These last two weeks I have to work full time at the orphanage. The first two weeks were somewhat boring with mostly coloring and sitting around watching the children. Just recently, they seem to be warming up. Now when I arrive they say "hello" and run up to me, give me hugs, and show me this or that. They even fight over who gets to hold my hand when we go for walks. Today, Alla ran over to me and was eager to show me a picture of her grandmother holding her when she was baby. She was so excited! The other children wanted to see it and she was closely guarding it. If you remember, Alla is eight and the oldest. She is very smart and eager to learn English. She is also the boss of the TV; deciding what to watch and when to watch it. Today, "Snow White" was on again.

Outside, there are swings, a play set, sand box, and two covered verandas. Today, Alla taught us to play hopscotch. I never knew it involved throwing a stone and then hopping to and from the point where the stone landed.

One day, Steve and I went to the Italian restaurant Napoli. We had the business lunch: all you can eat for 400 rubles. It was good. I had vegetable lasagna, pasta, chicken, and even French fries. I found it amusing, French fries! I had not had any in over a month. Back at work, a stray dog found his way into the playground. The kids loved this and chased it around for the longest time. One of the workers gave it some bread, but it would not eat it. He occasionally drank water from puddles and continued jumping on the kids and running around. Some excitement for the day!

Today, I decided to walk home from the orphanage instead of taking the bus. Although it poured and my sneakers were soaked, it was nice and cool and I felt refreshed. I was proud of myself being able to navigate myself home. Two hours in the rain!

When I arrived at work, the children were watching "Lilo and Stitch." The workers were taking the children's temperatures. There was another woman, perhaps a nurse, checking the kids over. I asked if someone was sick and Alla said that there was a stomach sickness going around.

Today, the women wanted to pick up something, so we took eight kids for a walk. It was stressful navigating the Novgorod streets with all the traffic and eight little kids. While one of the women went to pick up the stuff she was buying, we noticed some chickens in someone's yard. They were fenced in, but the children were curious. I had not come across anyone with farm animals in the city, so it was interesting to me, also. Along our walk, we saw a sports stadium used to house racehorses and a car mechanic's garage.

On Denis's 6th birthday, Francesca and I were given a cupcake to celebrate with everyone.

Usually I am doing homework when Olga takes Beesha for a walk, but this evening I decided to go with Olga. She walks him behind the building where there is much open space and more complexes with more housing. Olga talked with a man who lives in the building next to ours. He was eager to talk to me in Russian and complemented my speaking. From here, we walked to another building and went inside to visit. One of Olga's relatives and her brother and sister-in-law were here also. Olga's brother was helping remodel and putting a new floor down. I did not realize Olga had relatives living so close. For dinner, Olga cooked an American meal…pork chop, mashed potato, salad. During teatime, Olga introduced me to a drink called chesnok. It is strictly a Russian thing and looks like egg nog, but has a distinct taste of its own.

Today, I took my camera to work and took pictures of the kids. Alla wanted me to take pictures of only her. Along with this, I read a book to Alla about a princess, played blocks with Daniel, and accompanied the children as they discovered some ant farms. Work is enjoyable now, as a high level of trust is established between them and us.

Around 5:30, some parents come to pick up their children. Alla's mother showed up and was sitting in a swing talking to Alla. Lena told me she is a bad woman because she drinks a lot, has no job, but many different boyfriends. Lena told me most of the children's parents are in the same category. They drink, do drugs, and usually do not have a steady job. It is a sad situation and I think about kids in America in the same conditions. The orphanage must be their only security, because I cannot imagine what their home life is like.

## E-MAIL: WEDNESDAY, AUGUST 5, 2009 1:34 AM

Hi Mom, That was a very nice message. I appreciate the things you have told me about seeing me growing. It means a lot to know you think these things about me and see changes. I see myself going in many directions, too. I just don't know yet how I am getting anywhere. I do plan to stick with Russian class for at least another year at Brockport. After that, I do not know where I would be taking them. Olga says she hopes I come back someday, visit her, and go to Moscow. I told her I plan on doing that, as well as adopting a child or more. Knowing that I want to do all this, it is important for me to stick with the Russian language. Most of the group left today and from now on, I have internship 8 hours a day. Without class and homework, I will have more time to spend with Olga. This weekend we are going to stay in the Village where her mother and family live. I am excited! Sounds like you are keeping yourself busy. I got my computer working again. Thanks for keeping my school affairs in order and paying for everything.

This trip has certainly taught me so far that I am able be on my own and manage, somewhat. As for growing spiritually, I would agree, I have done a lot of that in the last 6 months. It has helped me deal with being away from home. I was only anxious when I first was dropped off. I guess I surprised myself or do not give myself enough credit. Kevin is doing well. I am sure he has told you what he is doing; he said he saw you the other day. He just recently started reading the Bible. It seems he and I have had an interesting summer of growing. I think this separation has done well for our relationship.

Be sure to tell everyone I say "hello." I am glad you got the postcard. Joseph should be getting one. My bank account is probably around 250 now, but I have finished buying all my gifts. I help Olga with dishes, but she will not let me do much. You have my return flight times and information. Not much time left! See you soon! Love, Sasha

## GOING TO THE VILLAGE: OLGA'S MOTHER'S HOME:

When I got home and ate, Olga announced that she was leaving soon for the village. So I packed my book bag and headed out the door. Olga and her aunt (mother's sister) and I along with the two pets, Beesha and Shira, squeezed into Olga's little red car. Shira sat between Olga and her headrest the whole trip. Beesha sat in the front.

The Village was a nice 2-hour ride through the lovely countryside. Some roads were so bad we had to drive on the shoulder. Some had potholes the size of Texas. When the road was not too bad, Olga stepped on the gas at 100km. I noticed many of the houses in the Village were painted nice bright colors: blue, green, yellow, and even pink. Olga's mom's house was green. This is where Olga grew up. Also, inhabiting the house are two dogs, cats, chickens, and bees. I got a quick tour of the inside and outside and was hungry…it was around 9:00 pm. Olga said I could not eat until after I went in the Banya.

## TO THE BANYA:

Banyas are a story in themselves. I found out that the farmhouse was built by Olga's grandfather, the father of her mother. In front of the house is a huge fenced in area where vegetables grow, a little house for tomatoes, four beehives, and many apple trees. Connected to it on the side of the house is an enclosure for chickens.

Banyas are strictly a Russian thing and Olga's mom said I had to experience a "Russian Banya", as well as a "Russian village." Toilets and showers are not in the same area and in the village, most people do not have a shower, but a banya. The banya is a small building with a small room and a larger room. You enter the small room first, take off your clothes, and go into the larger room, where there is a stove, a large basin of water, and some smaller basins you fill with water. There is a tiny platform to lie on and tiny benches. It is like a sauna, but a lot hotter. Anyways, Olga and I went in together…a bit awkward at first with no clothes on. There was only one light so it was pretty dark. When we went in, Olga put more water in the stove, causing the area to steam up. You start sweating a lot. I remember trying to breathe in and it was difficult. Then Olga had me lie down and she took a bunch of branches with leaves on them and hit me with them in a gentle, massaging fashion. You do this lying on your back and stomach and it actually feels nice. The second set of braches came from pine trees, was scratchier, but felt great. After this, you move to a bench. Olga asked if I wanted my hair washed. I said "yes": so she put shampoo and conditioner on my head, and then poured water from the basins on me. It felt really nice. After hair washing you take these big scrubbing things and scrub yourself down with soap. Olga poured more water on me and it was finished. Liza says that people can spend a whole day in a banya just talking and relaxing with friends. It feels so relaxing and refreshing...you could go to sleep.

Another thing, the banya is 50 feet from the house down a few stairs in an area of trees. I wonder how it is in the winter going to and from the banya? For the toilet, it looked like it used to be an outhouse, but now it has a toilet seat over the hole.

After the banya, we all had dinner. I noticed that everyone seemed to be yelling when they talked to each other. I do not know if this is because they cannot hear well or because it is just their norm. For dinner, we had fish, cabbage pie, and another meat that looked like pork chop, potatoes, tomatoes, and cucumbers. I was tired, but we had tea. Olga and the rest of her family were taking shots of cognac and grandfather tried to get me to have some. I went to bed and Beesha curled up next to me.

I love the Village. It is so quiet; I can hear the birds singing, the bees buzzing, the mosquitoes, the flowers swaying in the wind. I can feel the sun and a breeze on my skin. Every day, occasionally, you hear an alarm in the distance signaling a train is coming and soon it passes through. It reminds me of summer days at my own grandmother's house out in the country.

## THE CEMETERY:
I slept until 9:30. We had leftovers for breakfast. We all piled into the car and were on our way to the cemetery. The cemetery was in the middle of a bunch of tall grass with an

open space for the cemetery. We visited the burial places of Olga's grandparents, great grandparents, and her father. Olga's aunt and mother were cleaning the graves by brushing away dirt and leaves and cleaning the headstones. They also left cookies, candies, chocolate; and bread near, or on, the graves on stands located throughout the cemetery. I am sure it is most likely a customary thing to leave something for the spirits, but I am not sure. Overall, I felt privileged that they would bring me to the cemetery...such a private thing. The setting was very intimate; the trees in the wooded area were very pretty. Some older graves were very intricate with decorations. We came across a section for soldiers that served in World War II and the grave of a famous General from Novgorod, who has a street named after him.

When Olga comes to the Village, she does a lot of odd jobs around the house. Upon returning from the trip to the cemetery, I relaxed, mostly watched Olga, and took some pictures. We had borsch for lunch.

Later on, I wondered what Olga was up to now and looked out the front windows. I saw Olga and her mother dressed up in their bee outfits, extracting honeycombs from the hives. I found great enjoyment in watching them, because it reminds me of watching my own father at home do the same with his bees. I decided to go outside and watch from a closer distance. Bees were flying everywhere. A bee came out of nowhere, ran into me, and stung me in the neck. He then was stuck in my necklace. Olga came over and picked him off me. She also spit on her fingers, dabbed the sting, and said a line of something three times. I have no idea what she said....maybe a prayer. A few minutes later, grandmother came over and gave me some mint leaves to put on the sting. The leaves stung, but the bee sting never swelled.

I lay down and slept for quite a while. Grandmother said I was tired because I got stung. We then watched a TV program about a church and its icons. It was in English, dubbed in Russian, but you could still hear the English. Eventually we ate dinner. Chicken and pasta with vegetables. With tea, I had vanilla ice cream. After dinner, I spent the evening watching Zoo TV, again in English with Russian voice over it. It was a program about red pandas and hedgehogs. Everyone sat down for tea and took turns using the banya. Olga and I were the last to use it. It was not as hot as the night before, but just as relaxing.

I remember many people riding their bikes, families outside, children playing, many random dogs running around. Another thing that impressed me was that every house in the Village seemed to have its own fenced in area for raising their own food. The people are very capable of making it on their own; even in a crisis, as Stas had told us in history class. Some of the houses in the Village look so worn and I realize they are probably very old and it makes me wonder how the people survive in the wintertime. I noticed in our house there was a wood stove in the middle of the house, but I really wonder how they survive the harsh winters.

Olga and I spent the evening relaxing. For dinner, she made potatoes and mushrooms (sautéed in the frying pan with lots of butter). The next day we slept in again. For breakfast, we had these really good muffin things. They reminded me of English muffins at home, but they were filled in the center. There were three kinds: berries, potatoes, and cheese. Before eating them, Olga insisted on putting loads of melted butter on them. Very good! Potato is my favorite. I spent most of the day outside watching what Olga was doing. Last night she had started cutting grass and today she finished. I offered to help rake up the cut grass, but she never wants me to help.

Over the weekend, I finally finished reading, My Stroke of Insight. A great book!

On the way back home, Olga's aunt and uncle came with us. They are the ones who live a few buildings over from Olga. The ride home did not seem as long or as bumpy. For dinner, Olga made what looked like hamburger with noodles and vegetables. We spent some time talking about what kinds of books, food, and music Olga and I like. Olga said some of her favorite foods include fruits, meats, vegetables, and salted fish pie. As for music: Bach, Beethoven, Chopin, and Tchaikovsky. Classical is her favorite, but she does not like Rachmaninov because she says, she likes "nice music." I was surprised because Rachmaninov was born in Novgorod.

Olga loves to read, which is obvious if you see all her bookshelves. One of her favorite writers is Chehov. She loves history and classical books. Surprisingly, she does not like Tolstoy.

We went to the store across the street because Olga had to bake a cake the next day for a friend at work. The store was small, but cashiers get to sit. I am jealous because I have to stand while I am at work as a cashier. When we came back, I watched Olga make her cake and started reading the Unbearable Lightness of Being by Milan Kundera. I was surprised that Olga knew of the author, although he is from Prague. It is a good novel so far.

The batter Olga used to make the 6-layer cake looked like cookie dough and had a honey flavor. She took lots of lemons and shredded them whole, added sugar, cooked it, and spread it on top of the layers. She also had a saucer of milk and a whole block of butter cooking. I went to bed at 12:00 and she was still waiting for the milk stuff to be the correct consistency and was adding other things to it. She said she finished at 2:00 and had 6 hours sleep.

The kids were active as usual today. Daniel demanded that I push him a lot on the swings. He asked me to pick him up and carry him around and when I do, he tries to kiss me. I played kickball and catch with Veka and Allosha and then we jumped rope. I ate lunch with Steve, so we discussed the games he was playing at his work, as we listened to some music. I had a small container with Olga's cake in it. She had packed it for Steve and me. Returning from lunch, I did a puzzle with Anna and arts and crafts the rest of the time.

Some people showed up and I figured out that it was Allosha's mother, father, grandmother, and uncle. His mother looked young, the grandmother looked like she spends most of her time drinking; the uncle looked like he was in a daze. The father stood off to the side, separate from the others, was drunk with a beer bottle in one hand and a cigarette in the other. He mumbled something, and then sat on the street curb.

From what I could see, Allosha's mother squatted in front of him crying. The grandmother acted as if she had not seen him in a long time. I was surprised that the other children showed up and stood around watching. Allosha did not seem like he was interested. He was not upset, he just did not respond at all. The whole situation was interesting and strange. It reminded me of what Lena told me, that most families are drunks. I started thinking this explains why the children act the way they do. Lena had said that Allosha was a very good little boy. For the most part, he was laid back, does not cry or cause trouble. Some of the others constantly want attention, do not listen; or kick and hit each other. I feel sad for these situations…for all the kids.

Today, two new kids show up. A small girl named, Christina, and a boy named, Sameer. Sameer looks a lot bigger than the older children do. Christina has short boyish hair and the workers were checking her for lice. I wonder if she has been in another orphanage.

At home, Olga stuck a roasting chicken in the oven to bake while we took Beesha for his walk. We had potatoes and salad with it, yummy! After tea, I brought out my computer and let Olga pick out the pictures she wanted. I will have them made up for her before I leave. She also wanted pictures of Kevin and my Mom.

When I came home from work today, Olga was getting dinner ready quickly because she said she was going to the dacha. I told her I wanted to go and she said it is dirty and I would not like it. I begged and she finally said I could go.

## TO THE DACHA:

It was only about 10 minutes away, but the street we turned onto that had all the dachas was as bad as a country road. It was on the outskirts of the city. There was a long road with roads coming off it and dachas everywhere. A dacha is a small hut or house, on a piece of land, fenced in. Olga's little house was big enough to have two rooms; one had a small bed, a couch, and a table. The other was her banya! Wow! Olga has a banya at her dacha! She had to pick some onions. There were rows and rows of different plants; a small area covered for tomatoes. It reminded me of her mother's land in the Village. She told me to go for a walk. We were there about two and a half hours and the mosquitoes were coming out. I was glad Olga allowed me to come. On the way home, we noticed a woman waiting at a bus stop. Olga picked her up, drove her into the city a little ways, and dropped her off in front of housing buildings. Olga said she did not know the woman, but it was late and knew the buses do not come out here very often, it was getting colder, and she did not want her waiting. I thought how sweet it was of her to do that. I went to bed early. I liked the dacha and the fact that the people grow their own crops. I want to have something like a dacha and a banya!

While I was waiting for the bus, I saw an old woman with purple hair. Last night on my way home I noticed a car that had a plate that said "1<3 My American Car." It did not look like an American car. I chuckled. Under many of the signal lights, a timer counts down how many seconds until it turns green or red.

I watched some of my favorite movies: "Elizabethtown" and "Little Miss Sunshine."

## THE TOP TEN THINGS I WILL MISS ABOUT RUSSIA:

1. Olga, and her cooking.

2. Beesha and Shira.

3. Being able to walk around the city endlessly.

4. Food ... Olga's and all the Russian cuisine.

5. Architecture of Russia; especially Novgorod.

6. Clouds; they are massive.

7. Public transportation.

8. The Orphanage and the children.

9. The cats! So many.

10. The Russian people I have met and the ones I have become close to.

## SATURDAY, AUGUST 15TH:

Grandmother (Babushka) stayed at Olga's with me while Olga was away. I could hear her in the kitchen making pelmeni and noodles for later. We sat together while I ate. I asked her how her husband died and from what I understood, he had a heart attack at least 20 years ago. She, herself, had been a doctor for 46 years, her patients were small children. She was glad I am going to be a nurse. Now she receives a small pension. She said that in Russia, it is hard to find jobs and the pay is very small. She does not have a car now that she does not have a job so she takes the bus to Novgorod when she visits. She asked about my family; about my Mom and Dad. She gave me a small wooden plaque with Saint Alexandra on it. I asked to take a picture of her and me: she said, "Certainly." She is so sweet. Such a nice lady. I finished watching Click, and started reading a new book, My Sister's Keeper.

At work, we played outside for the last time. The staff was eager to talk with Francesca and me. We sang them the national anthem and a couple patriotic songs that we knew. They told us that they think Americans are good. Alla and Olga said we were wonderful girls and hoped each of us had a newfound appreciation for their culture. We exchanged e-mails and goodbyes. Alla told me to have a happy marriage and many kids. She hoped we would come back to Russia again and told me. "I will await you." she says this a lot when we leave work. The children were busy and waved "goodbye." The experience in the orphanage was great. The only thing I do not like is, I will never find out what happens to these kids. I hope they will have successful lives, a good job, and an education.

Steve came over in the evening and we watched a new Angelina Jolie movie, "Watchmen."

Stas had about 2,000 rubles (60 dollars) Liza left for the group to spend. Stas says, "Let's go out." We went for pizza at our favorite pizza shop. They had a pizza called, Obama Pizza. Stas, Adrian, Steve, and I ordered three Obama pizzas, three milkshakes and later three more, and another pizza; also a bottle of champagne. Stas and Steve discussed politics. Stas pointed out some different mannerisms between Russian and

American people. When Russian people smile, they do not show their teeth. They think that smiling without reason means you are stupid. Another thing, when Russians talk to you they get very close to you and this is not seen as being aggressive or in your space. 48 days coming to an end!! I can't believe it!

## MONDAY, AUGUST 17TH:

My last meal with Olga was mushrooms with vegetables, then a meat pie and a pork chop. Too much food! However, Olga said I would eat badly the next day so I had to be filled. After tea, she asked me what I wanted to do. I said I wanted to walk in the Kremlin one last time; in the rain. Therefore, that is what we did. I love cities at night and walking in the rain. It was perfect: Beesha, Olga, and me.

## TUESDAY, AUGUST 18TH: HOMEWARD BOUND:

My last morning with Olga was good. I got up at 5:15 am, got ready, took a shower. My favorite breakfast of blini filled with vegetables greeted me. I had my last cup of tea and we walked out the door. It was sad. The bus finally came to pick me up. Olga waved to me through the window until I could not see her any more. I could tell she was crying. The bus pulled away; I was crying too; I am going to miss so much. I cried again, when the plane left Russia and again right before we landed in NYC.

In NYC we ended up sitting on the plane for two and a half hours because of severe thunderstorms, before we could take off for Rochester and home; 561 lightning strikes in one hour. At one point, we could look out the window and see the crazy lightning all around us; kind of cool.

We finally arrived and it was nice to see my parents and my cat again. I want to end by saying thank you to everyone who has followed this journey with me and spent time reading this. Thanks to my parents for giving me this opportunity, Liza for all her work, and my fellow friends on the trip for great times. Last, but not least, thank you dearest Russia. You are beautiful!

# 8

## THE JOURNEY CONTINUES

After returning from Russia, Alex had two weeks to readjust to being home again and prepare for her fall semester. In her fall semester she took: Russian, Medical Surgical Nursing I, Fundamentals of Nursing, Health Assessment, and Math for Meds. Second semester found her taking courses in: Maternity, Medical-Surgical Nursing II, and Pharmacology. Of her experience with maternity she writes: "I was in the Special Care Nursery and spent the first part of the day holding and feeding babies. It is such a thrill to sit and watch these newborns sleep. Later on in the day, I was called into an emergency Cesarean-Section. The reason was because the baby's heart rate had dropped and not returned to baseline. When I arrived, the mother was getting put under. The baby was born within two minutes. A boy, with a large cone-shaped head. I was given the job of doing the first assessments on the newborn. The father came in and when he saw his son, he started crying. He shook when he cut the cord. It was at this moment that I felt very deep inside that I want to do this. The moment the father saw his baby, he loved him. Immediately. It was miraculous! The baby wasn't the cutest with his cone shaped head, yet, the parents loved him instantly. Later, I was told this is the love God has for each of us.

None of us is perfect, yet God loves us as we are. During this clinical experience, I was relaxed and confident. I left work feeling so happy and blessed. God is slowly showing me that there is more to life than grades and tests. While I need these to advance, there is so, so much more.

## AN UNFORGETTABLE DAY

Two weeks before Alex's 22nd birthday, Kevin came to our house to talk with us while Alex was at work. He had won an award of money at the University and had bought an engagement ring for Alex. They had been dating for four years. It was time to make a commitment. He did not know, at the time, when or how he would give it to her. He discussed his job interviews and graduation coming up in May. He asked for our blessing. It was to be a secret.

He decided that her birthday would be the day. When she told her closest friends, that Kevin had proposed and she had a ring, they said she should write all the details of how he proposed and send it to everyone. Because she is a good writer, I choose to use part of her description here:

Dear Friends,

Most days are unremarkable. February 16, 2010, was a Tuesday and my 22nd birthday. My mother had an appointment in Cleveland, so my parents left town and I was finishing a large paper due for nursing the next day. It was also Kevin's older brother's birthday and plans were for me to go to their home in the evening for dinner. Kevin called and insisted that I pick him up at the University of Rochester... he would pay for gas. I picked up Kevin and he insists on driving. I told him I wanted to drive, but he said that was too bad. As we are driving, I start questioning him about where we are going. He just says he is taking the long way home, but I know we are going in the opposite direction from home. I call Daniel, a friend of Kevin and say Kevin is getting us lost. Daniel just told me to go along for the ride and not worry about it. I start thinking of all the people that I know from Fairport. Over the past year, Kevin and I have been going to Fairport on weekends for Bible Study with friends of ours. We have made some amazing friends and had good times there. Daniel was one of those friends. We had passed all our favorite hangouts. We get closer to Fairport.

"Are we going to the canal?" We pull into the parking lot by the canal. Right before we get out of the car I go, "Are you going to propose to me? No, don't get your hopes that high!"

"We have to walk down the path and find everyone," he says. Therefore, we walk along the canal. The canal and trees had quite a bit of snow on them, as did the surrounding buildings. Christmas lights were still up, big snowflakes were falling, it was cold, and there were some clouds overhead. Quite pretty! We get to a bench, there are no people around, Kevin sits, and says for me to come and sit. Then he stands up, then down on one knee and starts his whole speech. He said when we met, he was 8 days late for my birthday, but this time he did not want to be late. I interrupt with, "Is this a joke?" He says no, it is real. I started crying as he is looking at me. He says, "Please don't cry." He tells me all these nice things. I interrupt again with, "Does my Mom know about this?" "Yes." So at the end of his speech he says, "I choose YOU, will you marry me?" I say "yes" and am so excited, super hyper, and giggling. I could tell from the tone of his voice, he was nervous and serious: a voice I had never heard before. We have spent many summer evenings getting ice cream, walking, talking, and watching the ducks along the canal. I had never been here in winter. I had told him when he did propose I wanted it  to be special in meaning. I must say, Kevin, you succeeded! Kevin came to my house about two weeks ago and talked to my parents. Therefore, our parents and his little brother were the only ones who knew. On the way home he told me how long he had been agonizing over the whole process and the story behind it. We had been talking about engagements and weddings a lot lately. Many of our friends were getting engaged/married soon and I wished that were us. I had asked Mom, questions about weddings. Then I would say, "This is ridiculous. It's Kevin who has to propose first." In March we will have our fourth anniversary of knowing each other and we are both ready to move to the next stage of this relationship. Kevin graduates this May and I graduate next May. As I write this, I look at my hand and let me tell you, it is still unreal! A real ring on my finger! These events make me feel older, more adult, but it has not sunk in yet. For all of you who are wondering, we plan to get married in 2011 or 2012. Spring is my favorite season. It will be at my Church, St. Joseph's... reception no idea. So thank you all who wished me a happy birthday and congratulations. Your well wishes mean a lot to me. To Kevin: Thanks for making me the happiest person in the world. I cannot wait to be married to you! I love you; you are perfect!

## MOVING ON WITH THE FLOW OF THE JOURNEY

Another phase of growing up and maturing is manifesting itself, as Alexandra makes more plans for her future. There will always be change. It is fact of life. I see magazines appearing in our home on how to have a simple wedding; mixed in with her anatomy and nursing books. She is looking forward to her clinical experiences in Nursing and her future with Kevin.

"My goal in Nursing is to be a Certified Nurse Midwife. I had this idea even when I switched my career from Physician Assistant to Nursing. It is such a thrill to see the instant love parents have for their children and to experience the miracle of birth."

As M. Scott Peck writes in The Road Less Traveled: "Life is difficult. This is a great truth, one of the greatest truths... because once we truly see this truth, we transcend it. Once we truly know that life is difficult... once we understand and accept it... then life is no longer difficult. Because once it is accepted, the fact that life is difficult no longer matters." Beyond this, there is only Faith, Hope, and Charity; as we thank, trust, and serve God in our life's journey.

# APPENDIX

## Poetry By Alexandra Genter

## A BLESSING

May you always get what you deserve
May you prosper all your days
May you always be smiling
May you find comfort in your life.

May you not be troubled
As you go through life
May your feet stay strong.

May you always be able to find your way
If the road gets get dark and narrow
If you stumble on your way
May you know that it is OK.

Find your voice and proclaim it proud

The stars are always within your reach
That's why they shine so bright
They are yours for the taking
Nothing is impossible with your head up.

I hope you are always happy
I hope you are always laughing
I hope you are always smiling.

# AWAKE

I awake this day; the sun rises
Oblivious around me.
Who am I?  I am just me.
As the sun rises and sets in familiarity
I am more puzzled;  I am just me.
Bright and early morning awaken in me
Journey outside my window
Foretold happenings lead me to believing
And I am just me.
The silence, it engulfs me, in my mind, all noise.
The light shines through the clock, it's ticking
The clouds, born of chaos, not knowing what they'll be
I wander like a cloud, in and out, and wonder what am I to
be?
I am just me.

# BIRTH MOTHER

Green and yellow shoes
Blue and white striped dress
The only remnants of an unremembered time and place.
Where a little girl began her life
Filled with uncertainty, questions, and confusion.

Mother, if you saw me now
What would you say?
Would you be pleased?

Look at what you abandoned,
Never looked back at what you never loved…
But, perhaps you did it out of love.

If only I could remember the places of my origins..
What I really am; who I really am.

And, Mother, I wonder what I am to you, if anything.
If you even remember..
I just wonder why?

As I look back at that little girl
Is she anything like you, mother?
Mother, who are you. You are a part of me.

Thank you, mother, for this life.
I shall show I am wanted
I shall have a purpose, I shall always try harder
I shall become ten times what you were
I am already……Thanks, Mother.

# BREAK IT DOWN

Break it down, just feel it, the complexities of science
Not as hard as you might think.
Don't let anyone let you think you aren't capable.
Our designs are nothing new.
My words are just symbols for concepts and meanings
Symbols on a page we give meaning to.

Does the meaning give it life?
Post the idea; context.

What is anything on this earth?
I am as real as the flesh on my skin
My hollow heart just pumping out blood
And the neurons in my brain making connections.

Just break it down; nothing more than symbols
Beat, beat, beat!
The beginnings will always be beneath the core of being
It's all perception.

# FAR AWAY AND I

How about me?

How can I stay inside this skin?

There is a lot of beauty outside.

In a far away place in the past

There was a little girl

Alone in a big world

She would play pretend with the thoughts in her head

Outside the window would I look

And far away I could see the world from the window.


Little feet traveled far away

I am here now

Play pretend now with the dog and the cat

Not so alone now.

On the swing, far away and up high

In the backyard, play pretend with the big trees

Pretty tall companions

Play hide and go seek, they are my protection.

Far, far the woods behind the lawn

Long walks and dark nights

The stars looked down shining at me

Could hear the frogs and crickets sing.

Far, far away, older now

Play pretend with thoughts in my head

Friends did come and go, some to stay.

The little girl; still little, deep inside

Far, far away are dreams she has inside

Far away, is there anything up above?

I say a prayer.  If God can hear me, it's a long shot.

I don't know what to expect in this life I'm living

There are too many ways to go

Those I've passed along the way

Close companions meet me in the night

In the light we'll stay together and pretend we're close forever.

The girl does not know where to go from here

Skin worn and dry, still thinking, still wondering....

Who am I supposed to be?

# I MET A BOY

I met a boy who had a passion for the Bills

With a wardrobe to reflect it.

Who would sit quietly longing to speak out,

So, instead I spoke.

He would sit and smile, listening intently

I met a boy who held things inside

And so I let him know what I saw in him from my eyes

He took things slowly but eventually opened up

He taught me all about 1st downs and running backs

How to understand fractions to quadratic equations to functions

Taught me that I am smarter than I feel.

I met a boy who did not believe in wasting the day away

Too much to see and do, can't miss the day.

I met a boy who always told me, you can do it; I believe in you.

I met a boy who finally saw me for me

And I didn't feel like I had to be anyone else

I met a boy who showed me that despite my flaws, I am beautiful.

I met a boy who believed the best day is spending a warm day

Fishing or golfing or taking in a beautiful ocean scene.

I met a boy who showed me the importance of family

Of being self-less without reservation…always being there

For others and lending a helping hand.

I met a boy and with him I shared my love of music, words, and nature

Of pictures and clouds and simple things of life.

And he shared his passion of video games and Bills

Of fun, adventure, taking things with a grain of salt and a bit of humor.

I met a boy who slowly took me away, with kind words and a nice smile

He opened my eyes to beauty and potential I had inside.

Together we opened each others eyes; we laughed and cried

And built a perfect something together.

I met a boy who taught me not to worry about trivial things

That the important things are being there, a gentle kiss and hug.

Without words, meanings can be heard in the silence and gesture.

I met a boy who enjoyed my simple definition of life, a country yard, a few dogs

I met a boy who taught me about love; not having to improve for someone else.


Love is an adventure to a new place; love is getting lost together

Love is the perfect dance under a starlight sky; a hum to the tune.


I met a boy.

# LOOKING GLASS SELF

I am a fragile person...

I think too much and worry even more

I hold on too tightly; afraid to let go.

Afraid to break like a China doll

And I look so together on the outside

But I am a labyrinth of emotion and wonder.

I'll be ok; I'll get by

Just need a little love and compassion to hold on to.

Hopefully, I won't smother it; I hope you understand

Why I am so afraid of being alone, so scared

But who isn't?

Not today.   I am stronger.


# CREATIVITY

On sweet creativity!

I feel you rising up,  I can.

Bursting from my soul

Heart pounding, eager to be free

With anticipation and excitement

From my fingertips

Traces released

And ever to be.

# UNTITLED

I don't know why I am so afraid of what is going to come one day.

When all the people will fade away; ashes are all that's left.

So I surround myself with photographs and tangible things

Just in case I ever forget.

I see I don't have enough of my parents; mother dear; father

My nose itches from all this commotion.

Why can't these be happy tears; breathe in, really deep

It is not happening now, so relax

I wish I had concrete proof and belief we will all be together some day

I will just cling to these pictures and believe it.

For a sense of comfort, can't we all rise and fall together. Not so alone.

Just so you know, for as long as I am able

I will think of you; you'll be on my mind

I'll wonder where you are, what you are doing; wherever you may be.

# CHAOS

If the walls were always moving, would I even notice?

Would I get lost in the every day hum drum of life?

Just like my footprints in the earth

Just like the pictures on the wall; like the order in the room

Maybe I should rearrange,  chaos is so much more

The dirt and specks on the floor; connect the dots.  Something new.

The lines in your skin, my favorite ones. Do you know them?

The chaos I appreciate, the stray hairs on ,my coat

Dust, oh dust!  Trails of neglect.

The words scroll across the screen, never ending, always changing.


And  oh!     New dots.   Let's connect.

# "MY JOSEPH"

## "MY BROTHER"

# "MY HOME"

*1992 - 1996*

*1996 - Present*

# "MY FAUN LAKE"

# "MY KEVIN"